*Twayne's English Authors Series*

Sylvia E. Bowman, *Editor*

INDIANA UNIVERSITY

G. K. Chesterton

G. K. CHESTERTON

# G. K. Chesterton

By LAWRENCE J. CLIPPER

*Indiana University at South Bend*

Twayne Publishers, Inc. :: New York

Library of Congress Cataloging in Publication Data

Clipper, Lawrence J.
    G. K. Chesterton.

    (Twayne's English authors series, TEAS 166)
    Bibliography:    p.
    1.  Chesterton,  Gilbert  Keith,  1874–1936.
PR4453.C4Z587                    828'.9'1209                    73-18048
ISBN  0–8057–1090–6

To My Mother

# Preface

If a substantial body of work were the only measure of great-
ness, Gilbert Keith Chesterton's place in literary history would
be assured. The first obstacle for anyone writing about Chesterton is the need to master his hundred-odd books, two-hundred
incidental essays and reviews, and the hundreds of still un-
collected periodical essays. The discussion is also complicated
by the bewildering diversity of Chesterton's interests and by
the various literary forms in which he worked: essays, reviews,
novels, poems, plays, biographies, histories—the list goes on.
The heterogeneity is even displayed in individual books, such
as the collections of essays pointedly titled *All Things Considered, All Is Grist, Generally Speaking,* and so on. The first
discovery that one makes about Chesterton, then, is that he
was an audacious and prolific polymath in an age of narrow
specialists.

Nor is the problem of quality any simpler. Thirty-some years
after his death, Chesterton's admirers, academic or otherwise,
are still unable to agree on which of his works are the most
important. Some prefer his romances, others his theological
books, some his social criticism, some his poetry, others his
literary criticism, and, perversely, a few those "tremendous
trifles," the innocuous and ephemeral journalistic articles churned
out during his thirty-year career on Fleet Street.

To create some order out of this mass and variety of material,
the working assumption adopted for this study is that Chesterton
is best studied as a man of ideas, not as an original thinker
certainly, but as a "contemplative" who believed that the most
important thing one could know about a man was his philosophy
of life.[1] He lived and breathed ideas, and he devoted a lifetime
to defending the rather unfashionable philosophy by which
he lived. That philosophy retains a remarkable unity, clarity,
and orderliness wherever it appears—and however it is displayed—in Chesterton's multitudinous works. What Chesterton

said of Hilaire Belloc and Leo Tolstoy may be applied with equal justice to his own ideas: that the reader always knew immediately what each would say on any given subject since "They do not form opinions, the opinions form themselves."[2]

The philosophical stance adopted by Chesterton early in his life and retained with unusual single-mindedness to the end was, in some ways, peculiarly English; in its delicate mixture of realism and mysticism it is reminiscent of Wordsworth, and, incidentally, also shows a poetic eye at work. More importantly, it rests in that great English literary tradition of Christian humanism that is best represented by John Milton, John Dryden, Alexander Pope, Jonathan Swift, and Dr. Samuel Johnson, all of whom were parts of Chesterton's early reading. Finally, his thought shows everywhere the stamp of St. Thomas Aquinas. Chesterton did not have to read the *Summa Theologica* in order to know the essentials of St. Thomas's synthesis, but he almost certainly had done so by 1908, long before he became a Roman Catholic convert. He might have found for himself the Thomistic element in Anglican theology and in the English humanistic tradition, or, being Chesterton, he would have eventually discovered for himself a form of personal Thomism. Whatever means of arrival at this position, it informs all that Chesterton wrote, including his political and social criticism and his later fiction and poetry.

Several subjects may be safely ignored in any study of Chesterton's thought. The first of these is a genetic account of Chesterton's ideas, and any related biographical or psychobiographical details. By 1900, the year he emerged into public view, his childhood, education, and milieu had already shaped him into the ruralist, radical, and orthodox Christian that he remained to his death. Chesterton was a man who lived his life almost entirely in his head, and indeed one may say that only three things "happened" to him in his life, and they served only to confirm him in his early beliefs.

The first event was his marriage in 1901 to Frances Blogg, which domesticated and protected the irresponsible, child-like man who could not tie his tie and often did not know in which city he was. The marriage also pointed him more surely in the direction of religious orthodoxy after a schoolboy flirtation with philosophical skepticism, solipsism, agnosticism, and Socialism. The second event was the Marconi trial of 1913, which resulted in his brother Cecil's being found guilty of libelling certain Jewish politicians and businessmen. Chesterton was permanently embittered by the outcome—exaggeratedly disenchanted considering the fact that Cecil escaped a prison term. The trial left him more than ever convinced that the Parliamentary system was corrupt and that English society was in the grasping hands of an international Jewish conspiracy. The third event was Chesterton's conversion to Roman Catholicism in 1922, a public declaration of spiritual attachments traceable in his earliest letters and essays. These three events, traumatic as they must have been, have in common the fact that they altered nothing in Chesterton's thinking; they merely confirmed his earlier thought and feeling.[3]

Other biographical details and their implications have been handled with tact and sure knowledge in Maisie Ward's excellent biography. And the problem of Chesterton's artistry, his prose style, his fiction, his poetry, can only be touched on in this study, leaving to the reader the joys of discovery and to other students the rewarding task of analysis.

I wish to thank Indiana University for the grant which permitted me to complete my work, and the research staffs at the Indiana University Library for their help: Larry Fortado in Bloomington; Mrs. Kathy Whitman, Mrs. Joan Falvey, and Mrs. Marsha Patterson at South Bend; and Mrs. Donna Harlan, IUSB Librarian, for unstinting aid. My thanks to Dr. Edward Wojciechowski for helping me through the thickets of Thomism, and Dr. John Cassidy, my colleague at South Bend, whose time-consuming efforts in reading and correcting the manuscript and numerous suggestions have served to guide me from egregious error.

Finally, I thank my wife for the proper mixture of encouragement and astute criticism while the work was in progress.

LAWRENCE J. CLIPPER

*Indiana University at South Bend*

# *Contents*

# Chronology

1874    Gilbert Keith Chesterton born May 29, Kensington section of London; first son of Edward Chesterton, retired house agent, and Marie Louise Chesterton (née Grosjean).

1887    January. Enrolled as day student at St. Paul's Preparatory School.

1892    Enters Slade Art School and also a period of skepticism and religious uncertainties.

1895    Leaves Slade Art School in the spring. Review of "The Ruskin Reader" in *Academy*, July.

1895-   Fleet Street period. Worked as sub-editor for two publishing
1899    firms; reviewed books and contributed poems and articles to several journals.

1896    Introduced to Miss Frances Blogg.

1899    Leaves Fisher Unwin. Settles on career as journalist and author. Moving toward Christian orthodoxy.

1900    First books published: *Greybeards at Play* and *The Wild Knight*. Meets Hilaire Belloc. As contributor to the *Daily News*, wins notoriety by his opposition to the Boer War. "Who is G. K. C.?" Campaigns for several Liberal candidates.

1901    January 6: begins Saturday column for the *Daily News*. June 28: marries Frances Blogg at St. Mary's Abbots, Kensington. *The Defendant*.

1903    *Robert Browning* for the English Men of Letters series. "The Blatchford Controversy" in the *Clarion* (to December, 1904).

1904    *The Napoleon of Notting Hill*.

1905    *Heretics*. September 5: begins weekly articles for *Illustrated London News* to be halted only by his death. Campaigns for Belloc and other Liberal party candidates.

1906    *Charles Dickens*.

1908    *The Man Who Was Thursday*; *All Things Considered*; *Orthodoxy*.

1909    *George Bernard Shaw*; *Tremendous Trifles*. The Chestertons move to Beaconsfield.

1911    Belloc begins *The Eye-Witness* (becomes *The New Witness* under Gilbert's brother, Cecil Chesterton, in October, 1912; G. K. Chesterton contributes to both).

1910   *What's Wrong With the World.*

1913   The Marconi affair. Chesterton severs connections with the *Daily News.*

1914   August 5: war with Germany. November: falls seriously ill; in a coma until March, 1915.

1915   Convalescing until June.

1918   November, after the Armistice, Cecil Chesterton dies in France.

1919   Trip to Palestine.

1920-
1921   The first trip to the United States.

1922   Edward Chesterton, Chesterton's father, dies. Gilbert K. Chesterton becomes a Roman Catholic on July 30.

1923   *The New Witness* dies. *St. Francis of Assisi.*

1925   March: *G. K.'s Weekly* started.

1927   Trip to Poland for one month. *Collected Poems.*

1929   Trip to Rome. *The Thing.*

1930-
1931   Second visit to the United States. Lectures at the University of Notre Dame.

1932   Attends Eucharistic Congress in Dublin. Begins series of radio talks on BBC.

1933   Mrs. Edward Chesterton, his mother, dies.

1934   Visit to Rome, Sicily, Malta.

1935   Trip to France and Italy.

1936   Visits Lourdes, and Lisieux, France. Taken ill. June 14: Dies. *Autobiography.*

1938   Frances Chesterton, Chesterton's widow, dies.

# CHAPTER 1

## Romance of a Man Reading

IN the spring of 1895, while still enrolled at the Slade School, the young Gilbert Keith Chesterton submitted his first article for commercial publication.[1] There is something poetically appropriate in the event, for the subject of this first effort was John Ruskin, former Slade Professor of Art at Oxford, and a Victorian whose career as a social critic had evolved, like butterfly from chrysalis, from his early interests in art and literature. Although Chesterton's writing career cannot be so neatly compartmentalized as Ruskin's (books on economics, politics, religion, and literature spilled from his pen with staggering unpredictability), it is easy to see that his career as a social critic was launched by his early years as a critic of art and literature.

Chesterton was, above all, a man of books—an indefatigable reader of novels, essays, classics, detective stories, and fairy tales. He could often be seen walking on Fleet Street totally absorbed in the latest detective story, while other cheap novels spilled from the folds of his Spanish cape. Like Thomas Babington Macaulay and Oscar Wilde, he had a phenomenal memory and could recite long passages from poems and novels read years before. Uniquely, he could glance through a book and extract without effort the main points of the author's argument. Reading Chesterton today, one can still be impressed by his ability to express with wit and accuracy the fundamental core of an artist's work and personality.

### I  Biases of a Critic

Chesterton's voracious appetite for reading and his keen discrimination of an author's logic were not always matched, however, by the spirit of generosity one expects in a great critic. For example, since he was incurably blind to the appeal of contemporary art and literature, he lashed the moderns with the pejoratives "Futurists" or "Post-Futurists." Wilde was a "charlatan," Ibsen was "splendidly wrong," modern paintings were "the latest artistic insanities," and most modern novels were impossible to read because of their "sloppy" formlessness.[2] One can admire the perspicacity of that master at St. Paul's who wrote on one of Chesterton's schoolboy reports, "Means well. Would do better to give his time to 'Modern' subjects."[3]

Chesterton's animus against modernism appears not only in his handling of individual artists but in the very premises of his critical work. His criticism appears to be unfashionable today because of these premises—the heavy emphasis given to moral and religious intent, the impressionistic style, the display of personal enthusiasms, and the frank prejudice in favor of clarity of form and theme. In fact, the constant moral vigilance of his criticism does more than anything else to alienate the modern critic from Chesterton. He himself never doubted the need for morality in art, even in those early days when, as a Junior Debater, he wrote a paper deploring "the absence of the sentiment of the moral" in modern literature.[4] As a mature man, that same schoolboy simply persevered in the war against "the tiresome half-truth that art is unmoral."[5] Against the doctrines of the esthetes of the Late Victorian period, Chesterton opposes the corrective notion—strange to modern ears—that the artist has nothing to write unless he has "his own theory of life which he thinks right, or somebody else's theory of life which he thinks wrong, or at least some negative notion that somebody is wrong in thinking it wrong."[6]

Even didacticism, anathema to modern criticism, becomes tenable from this presumption. Chesterton points approvingly to the timeless popularity of detective stories, fairy tales, and the novels of Dickens; and he explains that they have lived because such works are free of "the mean modern notion of keeping the moral doubtful."[7] Most of recent literature Chesterton consigns to an ashheap because it all lacks a "plan of the idea that is straight like a backbone and pointing like an arrow."[8] The modern writer, having lost his awareness of a meaningful universe must, according to Chesterton, wander through life creating purposeless, amoral, and meretricious works of art.

Chesterton's was a Puritan theory of art, of course; and it willingly jettisoned esthetic analysis in its concentration on the moral component in the created work and on the moral sensitivity of the creative artist. Indeed, the Puritan critic (Chesterton would have been distressed by the adjective) was driven to conclude that the creative act is valuable *only* for its inherent moral thrust; and Chesterton could conclude, therefore, that "the highest use of the great masters of literature is not literary; it is apart from their superb style and even their emotional inspiration. Literature, classic and enduring literature, does its best work . . . in balancing other and older ideas against the ideas to which we might for a moment be prone."[9]

In accordance with this view, Chesterton regarded his function as a literary critic "to be especially interested not only in the literature left by the man but in the philosophy inhering in the literature."[10] The modern critic may censure this pragmatic critical stance as the "intentional fallacy" or even dismiss it as puerile.[11] For all that, it is the major premise of all of Chesterton's criticism; and it gives unity to his book reviews, book-length literary studies, and his treatment of literary figures in such books as *Heretics*. Chesterton was indeed, as his brother asserted, "a writer on philosophical questions before he was a critic."[12]

There were moments when Chesterton realized that he was in a cul-de-sac with Plato, who had been determined to banish the poets from his Republic, particularly if they uttered seditious ideas. In one essay, Chesterton distinguishes between the morality an artist aims to teach and the "morality he takes for granted," those things "he forgets to explain."[13] The distinction is vague but seems to imply the difference between a conscious personal "message" and some unconscious, universally available "knowledge." "This thing," he continues, "which is deeper even than morality, which we may if we like call philosophy" is a human harmony or order latent in the work of art and discoverable to the sensitive critic. The distinction, however, is only a temporary escape from the Platonic dilemma; for the critic is still asked to rivet his attention on some intellectual or thematic content.

Also implicit in Chesterton's view of art is a democratic anti-

intellectualism and cultural despotism that are quite in harmony
with his general preference for the unwashed many over
the educated few. If Jacob Epstein's statues, for example,
are reviled publicly, it is because the common man is "not
stupid or blind or benighted."[14] The state is warranted in using
censorship or other controls to protect a decent citizenry from
the ever-present threat of seditious or irreligious art. Looking
at a recent work by some "futurist," Chesterton acridly remarks
that "a saner generation will cover up such a thing in shame."[15]
In *All Is Grist*, he proclaims the theory that if a work of art
is "really at enmity with morals . . . I am so old fashioned as to
think that it ought to be denounced and even destroyed as
such."[16]

## II   *Practical Criticism*

One discovers that Chesterton's dogmatism is sustained viscer-
ally rather than intellectually and that it does not prevent him
from creating a corpus of practical criticism which remains
unequalled for its essential rightness. One need not be puzzled
long by the apparent discrepancy between the brittle theorizing
about art and the endearing brilliance of most of what Chesterton
wrote about specific authors. Cecil Chesterton indicates the
essential clue when he says that his brother was "at his best
when he is analyzing a writer with whose root point of view
he is sympathetic."[17] His subjects—Robert Browning, Charles
Dickens, William Blake, George Bernard Shaw, Robert Louis
Stevenson, Geoffrey Chaucer—are generally yea-sayers, humorists
rather than tragedians, critics of their societies, lovers of humanity, and therefore mirror-images of G. K. Chesterton. At ease
with these friends and companions, and freed from the necessity
of defending a minority philosophical position, Chesterton could
act as a genial host at a literary feast attended by other robust,
sane-minded men. If the repast offended the delicate tastes of
some literary gourmet, so much the worse for his decadent soul.
These studies display the uniquely Chestertonian blend of
criticism. A rationalistic kind of criticism, it centers on the
author's ideas and philosophy; yet, paradoxically, it is personal,
enthusiastic, and quick to respond with the impression of the

moment. On this latter point, Chesterton asserted that the beginning of all criticism is "wonder combined with the complete serenity of the conscience in the acceptance of such wonders"[18]— perhaps an echo of Samuel T. Coleridge's "willing suspension of disbelief." These two strains in Chesterton's critical temperament explain why his criticism gravitates either to the analysis of theme and subject matter on the one hand, or to personal "appreciation" and the adulation of accepted classics on the other.

### III   Robert Browning

Chesterton's disregard for facts and his critical dependence on impressions and atmosphere are found in his first full-length study, *Robert Browning* (1903). The literary essays collected as *Twelve Types* (1902) had brought him to the attention of the editors of the English Men of Letters series, who honored the young man with the assignment for the Browning study. Far from being awed by this generous act, young Chesterton infuriated the editors and the Browning societies with a book which treated the facts with insolence and which careened recklessly from speculation to half-truth, to diatribes against other critics, and from one personal bias to the next.

In spite of the bravura performance, the book astonished the literary world and announced the arrival of a talented critic to be reckoned with. However, reading it today, one can easily see its numerous faults. It is totally unsatisfactory in its treatment of the individual poems (some of "the facts" that Chesterton was willing to ignore) and in its evaluations of them. Chesterton spends as much time on "Mr. Sludge the Medium" as he does on "The Ring and the Book," possibly because of his own hostility to Spiritualism. Many of Browning's most notable poems—"My Last Duchess," "Fra Lippo Lippi," "Andrea del Sarto," "The Bishop Orders His Tomb"—are barely mentioned, if at all. "Karshish" and "Cleon"—those poems of the Christian revelation that are so important to the modern reader—are neglected entirely; and "Saul" is treated only cursorily. One immediately suspects that Chesterton's own orthodox religious persuasions were a major obstacle to a more balanced treatment of these poems. Nor is he immune to reading his own ideas into the poems, as when he ignores the evidence within "Fra Lippo Lippi" to announce that Browning had a consuming hatred for "Aestheticism, Bohemianism, the irresponsibilities of the artist, the untidy morals of Grub Street and the Latin Quarter."[19]

Aside from these lapses of factuality and proportion, Chesterton's *Browning* is difficult to surpass, if only because he is able to present with great sensitivity some essential truths about the poet's thought and temperament. He follows (without properly attributing it) the line of argument suggested by Bagehot's earlier criticism of Browning: Browning's poetry has an element of "grotesque" energy that resembles life itself. This same grotesquerie one observes in the gargoyles of Notre Dame or in Gothic art generally; and it reflects the same optimism, the same love of life (149). This defense is less surprising than it must have been to the Edwardians, whose poetic standards were still defined by the example of Alfred Tennyson. Credit must be given to Chesterton for finding Browning's obscurity a virtue in itself; for him, as for Ezra Pound and T. S. Eliot, there was a charm about Browning's poetry arising from a "certain tormenting uncertainty" (158).

Chesterton is equally penetrating on matters of Browning's technique; indeed, he anticipates by several decades the work of a battery of literary critics. In contrasting, for example, the poetry of the eighteenth century, which Chesterton defines as words "spoken about a certain situation," and the poetry of the nineteenth century, which is often spoken by a fictional person "in that situation," Chesterton not only illuminates the once vexing problem of a speaking *persona* in the poem but also anticipates Northrop Frye's fruitful distinction between "literature as a finished product" and "literature as process."[20] Admittedly, these technical matters do not long delay Chesterton from his confrontation with Browning's ideas. The dramatic monologue does not reveal to Chesterton, as it does to Frye, the large implications arising from the shift from "a literature of being" to a "literature of becoming." To Chesterton, Browning's formal accomplishment is interesting to the extent that it is "the perfect expression" of modern democracy. All of his poems, especially "The Ring and the Book," express the multiplicity of truth and the richness of life; they reveal that "no man ever lived upon this earth without possessing a point of view" (171).

Chesterton hastens to reassure the reader that neither he nor Browning is a relativist, that the content of the poems is still the primary consideration. One may find it necessary "to listen to all sides of a question in order to discover the truth of it"; but, when the listening is finished, one is relieved to discover that "there was a truth to discover" (175). Chesterton is silent on the subject of the truth expressed in "The Ring and the Book," possibly because it is delivered by a somewhat Protestant Pope.

Browning's "truths" are spelled out quickly in Chesterton's final chapter. Lacking the completeness and subtlety of modern academic scholarship, Chesterton's *Browning* still succeeds in outlining the essential theses of Browning's philosophy—man's blessed imperfection, the necessity of struggling against evil, the goodness of life, and the pervasive optimism. One detects even in this sharply compressed summary a sufficient explanation for Chesterton's triumph with *Robert Browning*: the shared philosophy freed Chesterton to discover other virtues in the poetry—the realism, the attention to detail, the unabashed grotesquerie—that scholars have only recently begun to explore in depth. With the *Robert Browning* volume, Chesterton found a groove which he was never to leave and which accounts for many of his other successes as a literary critic.

## IV  *Dickens*

The one literary figure with whose name Chesterton's will always be linked is Charles Dickens. It is difficult to describe the complexity of their relationship. Chesterton wrote three books on Dickens, innumerable essays and reviews, referred constantly to him and his works while discussing tangential matters, was a president of the Dickens Fellowship, and once participated in a mock trial on the matter of John Jasper's crime against Edwin Drood. One may safely say that nothing else of Chesterton's literary criticism retains its vitality—its "potent and widespread" impact, as one critic says—as does his work on Charles Dickens.[21]

Paradoxically, the modern critics find Chesterton's enthusiasm and undisciplined analyses of the novels rather embarrassing; for, equipped with critical tools unavailable to Chesterton, the modern critic has unearthed with rigorous technique Dickensian riches that the earlier critic never imagined. About only one thing do they agree: a virtual flood of scholarly books, articles, anthologies, and editions has served only to vindicate the conclusion of Chesterton's *Charles Dickens* (1906) that Dickens's "place in nineteenth century England will not only be high, but altogether the highest."[22] To Chesterton's everlasting credit, he could foresee such a reputation at a time when Dickens's fame was at its nadir, when the Victorian novelist was considered by many as simply "vulgar and flashy."

On almost every other point, the modern critic has diverged from Chesterton's estimate. For example, since Edmund Wilson's seminal work in the 1940's, it has been fashionable to say that the later novels are Dickens's best work, that they are proof that he was alienated from a corrupt society, and that he was perhaps even a revolutionary or Marxist. A large part of Chesterton's efforts in *Charles Dickens* is spent proving that the earlier novels are the most delectable and that *Pickwick* is unsurpassable. (In a later interview Chesterton said that, if he were stranded alone on a desert island with one book, he should like to have Thomas's *Guide to Practical Shipbuilding;* if he were in no hurry to leave, it would be *Pickwick.*[23]) Quantitatively, *Charles Dickens* reveals where the critic's admiration lies: the six novels after *Bleak House* take up only thirteen pages, *Great Expectations* only two, and *Pickwick* twenty-seven! "Those who have any doubt about Dickens can have no doubt of the superiority of the later books. Beyond question they have less of what annoys us in Dickens. But do not, if you are in the company of any ardent adorers of Dickens . . . insist too urgently on the spendour of Dickens's last works, or they will discover that you do not like him" (181-82).

The "splendour" which Chesterton finds detrimental in the later books results from the novelist's having "diminished in the story as a whole, the practice of pure caricature. Still more coarsely it may be put in the phrase that he began to practice realism" (180). The early works vibrate with caricature, mythic vitality, and an esthetic freedom which gradually fade and are replaced by "characterization," restraint, and artistic discipline.

To Chesterton, the true Dickens may be defined as a creator of living characters, fictional creations pounding with a mythic intensity that lies beyond the cool grasp of a George Eliot or a William M. Thackeray. Chesterton finds in him an "ungovernable sense of life"; indeed, he is " 'like life' in the truer sense, in the sense that he is akin to the living principle in us and in the universe; . . . His art is like life, because, like life, it cares for nothing outside itself, and goes on its way rejoicing. Both produce monsters with a kind of carelessness, like enormous by-products" (17). (The reader may be reminded of the praise accorded Browning's "grotesque.") Dickens is, in short, a kind of god incarnating himself for a godless Victorian age: "The power which he proceeded at once to exhibit was the one power in letters which literally cannot be imitated, the primary inexhaustible creative energy" (77-78).

It is an error, says Chesterton, to categorize Dickens as a novelist. His characters are best seen as belonging in groups or episodes, rather than in novels. The novels flow into each other in a kind of phantasmagoria of living creatures that make up a fictional universe; they are themselves only so much "machinery directed to facilitating the self-display of certain characters," or, better, "simply lengths cut from a flowing and mixed substance called Dickens" (81). It follows that the early novels are especially vital in establishing Dickens's genius. With them, he made a "mythology"; with the later novels, he created more "realistic" or "lifelike" people, a lesser achievement (83).

Very little of this criticism appeals to the taste of the modern reader. It is unsettling to observe a critic waving his arms and leaping about with enthusiasm, and one does not feel enlightened to hear that Dickens is like life and that life is like exploding rockets and the tingling of nerves. It is more discomforting to hear that Dickens had "godlike qualities," that he was a "creator" who flung down Mr. Guppy "like a miracle from an upper sphere" (242). And one does not think much of literary criticism which concludes that "most hymns about God are bad; and this is why most eulogies on Dickens are bad."

Though such criticism is unthinkable in this more antiseptic

era, it is justifiable if one agrees that paeans are the proper
response to Dickens. Chesterton's criticism is indeed guilty of
lacking "discipline" and "textual awareness," but the unwavering
enthusiasm and the essential rightness of the larger conclusions
are impressive. At the least, Chesterton succeeds in the elementary duty of the critic: he makes his reader want to re-read
Dickens. Thus one wishes to check Chesterton's impressions
that Mr. Nickleby is "the truly great achievement" of *Nicholas
Nickleby* and that Mrs. Micawber is "very nearly the best thing
in Dickens." Beyond this reaction, the reader is made to examine
his own critical credo. Has one not, for example, lost something
valuable, perhaps fundamental, in relegating one's immediate
responses, one's enthusiasm, to a minor role in the act of criticism? In any case, Chesterton's final judgment on Dickens
remains unanswered and unanswerable; and it still provides
a valuable introduction to the subject.

Chesterton's defense of Dickens was continued in *Appreciations and Criticisms of the Works of Charles Dickens* (1911),
really a collection of the twenty-one introductions written for
the Everyman edition of the novels. The collection is naturally
more fragmented than *Charles Dickens* since the introductions
treat the individual novels as isolated works and lack any over-
arching thesis. Nevertheless, the thesis of the earlier study
surfaces occasionally in them: the reader once again is made
aware of the energy, vitality, the living truth of Dickens's
characters.

Still absent in the discussion are the benchmarks of modern
criticism of Dickens: the subtle readings of irony and ambiguity,
the collation of images and symbols, the oppressive gloom. The
essays argue for the "mythic" vitality of Sam Weller, Pickwick,
Pecksniff, Tiny Tim, and Quilp—all from the earlier books.
Typically Chestertonian is the essay on *Great Expectations*, one
which is wholly concerned with the doings of Trabb's boy, the
minor figure whose "rush and energy" and "bounce" is a dynamic
representation of the Englishman's traditional defiance of upper-
class values. (For those who may be offended by the impressionistic word "bounce," it may be pointed out that the eminent
critic E. M. Forster reluctantly concludes that the only way of

determining the worth of a novel is by the writer's ability "to bounce the reader into accepting what he says.")[24]

While not a piece of modern criticism, *Appreciations and Criticisms* offers some anticipations of contemporary treatments of Dickens. Chesterton adumbrates the dominant psychological view of Dickens by concluding that during the Warren's Blacking episode "in some psychological sense he had really been wronged." Chesterton, who senses Dickens's lifelong disaffection with Victorian culture, perceives that even the good times of *Pickwick Papers* are tainted by a more poisonous vision. Finally, when Chesterton observes that "in one very real sense style is far more important than either character or narrative," he—while refusing to follow his own clue—prepares the way for an army of modern critics who occupy themselves with the nuances of diction and style.[25]

Chesterton is like his hero, however, in that he scatters these insights broadcast without deigning to examine the potential riches within. His final stance *vis-à-vis* Dickens is one of critical quietism. "All the critics," he writes in the essay on *David Copperfield*, "when all is said and done, have only walked round and round Micawber wondering what they should say. I am myself at this moment walking round and round Micawber wondering what I shall say. And I have not found it yet" (139). Dickens, that "great Cockney," had always demanded "the supremacy" of humanity over the intellect. With that he had won the unrestrained, and uncomprehending, adulation of another Cockney who knew that the "most fastidious modern who ever dissected his grandmother" would never understand Dickens any better. Once Chesterton admitted that, the only appropriate attitude seemed to be worship: "There remains that primum mobile of which all the mystics have spoken: energy, the power to create."

## V  George Bernard Shaw

Perhaps the only other person of Chesterton's time who loved Dickens equally, if for different reasons, was George Bernard Shaw. This mutual interest in the great novelist at a time when Dickens's reputation was at low ebb was one factor which made bedfellows of Chesterton and Shaw, those otherwise dissimilar figures. Shaw was everything that Chesterton was not: Irish, Socialist, rationalist, Puritanical, and teetotalling. He was agnostic at first, but he eventually hammered out a personal faith in "the Life Force"—that "vast and universal church," said Chesterton, "of which he is the only member."[26] For years, in private homes, newspapers, and public halls, the two men debated the merits of religion, Socialism, Catholicism, feminism, and—most heatedly—the liquefaction of St. Januarius's blood, always inconclusively, but also without alienating each other. Chesterton said that "my principle experience, from first to last, has been in argument with him."[27]

The two remained friends and correspondents, defended each other from the common enemy, and dared to appear (on James Barrie's estate) in each other's presence in cowboy costume. The money-wise Shaw spent years giving Chesterton financial and legal advice, and urging him to write dramas—where money was to be made. In turn, Chesterton wrote a book about his friend which Shaw announced was "the best work of literary art I have yet provoked"—adding wickedly that it was also "madly wrong."[28]

No one would have predicted that Chesterton's *George Bernard Shaw* (1909) would be either accurate or sympathetic. The book was brought into the publisher's office chapter by chapter, often on scraps of paper, and with no visible signs of having been researched. On the basis of the public debates and the essay in *Heretics* (wherein Chesterton accused Shaw of ignoring all the facts of human history and psychology), one might reasonably have expected a thoroughly antipathetical discussion. Aside from the fact that Chesterton always treated his enemies with cordiality, the explanation for Chesterton's generosity in *George Bernard Shaw* lies in the fact that the two geniuses had much in common. First of all, Chesterton admired the Arnoldian quality of "high seriousness" in Shaw. Perhaps because he himself was frequently accused of being "only frivolous," he was intent upon showing that beneath Shaw's levity was a sober concern for England and mankind. Thus, Chesterton saw that, in spite of the "anarchy" (secularism) evident in Shaw's philosophy, he had accomplished what all great artists do: he had created a body of ideas to be considered—fortunately to be rejected—by his audience.[29] Chesterton's real appreciation of Shaw rests on Shaw's having made the drama philosophical rather than dramatic.

Linking arms with Shaw, Chesterton the Catholic moralist joins Shaw the Puritanical Socialist, the Right joins the Left, to announce that art's purpose is not art but the serious presentation of ideas. This large area of agreement perhaps explains why the book is organized more to analyze Shaw's ideas than his dramaturgy. The six chapter titles reveal the author's penchant for philosophy: "The Irishman," "The Puritan," "The Progressive," "The Critic," "The Dramatist," and "The Philosopher." Even the chapter on "The Dramatist" skirts the problems of dramaturgy and presents an analysis of Shaw's morality and religion.

The titles also reveal that Chesterton has discerned the main outlines of Shaw's philosophy and personality. If these insights seem less earthshaking than they once did, it is because they have by now, like coins, been dulled with years of handling. A multitude of scholars, amateur Shavians, and doctoral candidates (who can find in almost any of Chesterton's sentences the seed of a dissertation) have succeeded in verifying Chesterton's general conclusions, which now seem like commonplaces: that Shaw's outrage against modernism is partly a result of his Irish background; that his Puritan upbringing may be felt in every line he wrote; that his favorite author is John Bunyan; that his humor cannot conceal the *angst* that lies beneath the existential skin; that his ethics require modern man to be constantly aware of the significance of each act. (One facet of Shaw's work pointed out by Chesterton but not yet fully understood is Shaw's willingness to drudge through the city budgets, crime reports, sewage disposal plans, and all the other minutiae of Victorian city life, in order to sustain the theories of Fabian Socialism.) It is no surprise that Shaw the playwright is concealed in this cataract of information about the philosopher and ideologist.

Chesterton's affection for Shaw is also explained by their agreement on the larger purposes of human life—while they agreed to disagree about the means by which certain ends

are to be attained. It is surprising to discover just how wide
their area of agreement is: that poverty is the unforgivable
flaw in industrial society; that the importance of money should
be faced, but that human life is of paramount importance; that
man's lower passions had to be recognized before solutions
could be found for his difficulties; that Reason must be sub-
ordinate to the larger purposes of Life. Almost bemused by his
discovery of their accord, Chesterton confesses "I come at last
almost to agree with him" (172).

Finally, for all Shaw's errors, his saving grace has been his
continual affirmation of the dignity of the human race and the
power within man to shape his future. He is one of the small
band who fought the pessimism and determinism of the late
nineteenth century: "When the spirit who denies besieged the
last citadel, blaspheming life itself, there were some, there
was one especially, whose voice was heard and whose spear
was never broken" (190). In Shaw, Chesterton discovered that
a secularist might be an ally in the cause of Man.

## VI  *Other Individual Studies*

Before Chesterton embarked on his career as a literary and
social critic, he had to divest himself of his connections with
criticism of the art world. He did so with G. F. *Watts* (1904),
a small study of a respected but nearly forgotten portraitist of
the great Victorians. The volume is interesting because it raises
in a crucial form the essential problem of Victorian painting:
its literary content. Perhaps predictably it shows the young
Chesterton opting for the Victorian tradition rather than for
the purely visual or technical achievements of the moderns. For
Chesterton, the main merits of such paintings as "Death Crown-
ing Innocence," "Mammon," and "Eve Repentant," is that Watts
was "copying the great spiritual and central realities which
literary and philosophy also set out to copy."[30] "Mammon" is a
great painting because it is "obviously an attempt to portray
not a twopenny phrase but a great idea" (115). The critic's
weakness for allegory and didacticism, his strict literalness, and
his implicit attack on the Impressionists (rather unfashionably
since they had won their battle in the 1890's)[31] mark Chesterton

as a standard-bearer for the Victorian academic tradition. His decision to abandon a career as an art critic may have been the wisest he ever made.

Less wise was Chesterton's decision to write *Blake* (1910), the study of a figure whom he was almost certain to find uncongenial. Chesterton could tolerate Blake as a painter and engraver, but only by emphasizing his "Roman" qualities—that is, the same strong classical forms and the decision of outline which the critic found in Watts. Completely ignored in all of the discussion is Blake's visionary quality, his inventiveness (both technical and esthetic), his absorption in an interior world—in short, his imagination.

If Chesterton's neglect of the imagination is harmful in his treatment of Blake's work as an engraver, it is positively destructive in any discussion of Blake the poet. Chesterton's approach to the subject is best indicated by one of his chapter titles: "Was Blake Mad?" The answer is a qualified "yes": Blake's imagination and the religious "system" it spawned are subsumed as "spiritual communications" with "canaille spirits." Always a contender against Spiritualists, and mistrusting all varieties of eccentric Protestantism, Chesterton dismisses contemptuously all of Blake's accomplishments in symbolism and mythmaking, as well as the religious and political radicalism that is not completely unrelated to Chesterton's own thought.

Easier for Chesterton to write was *Robert Louis Stevenson* (1927), whose subject was a mirror-image, one might say, of its author. In their youth, both Chesterton and Stevenson had been solitary, thoughtful, and sensitive boys; and they had found their ease in a world of fairy tales and toy theaters. The critic sympathizes with Stevenson's having "barricaded himself in the nursery"; in so doing he was "trying to get home," finding his escape, making his attempt to avoid the ugliness of the modern world.[32] With a familiarity probably born of experience, the critic surmises that Stevenson's love of the toy theater explains his simple characterizations, stark conflicts, and unambiguous resolutions in his fiction. The critic also finds in Stevenson a compatriot in the struggles against estheticism, decadence, and nihilism at the end of the century. In spite of the similarity of the two men, there is much that is unsatisfactory about Chesterton's study of Stevenson. Perhaps it is that Chesterton is primarily interested in "the philosophy inhering in the literature," and that there is not much to be said about Stevenson's philosophy. Although the study has much charm and sympathy, its lack of tension or complexity renders it somewhat bland for modern tastes.

The dubious honor of being Chesterton's worst piece of literary criticism falls, however, to *Chaucer* (1932), which begins ominously with the pronouncement that "it is possible to know [Chaucer] without knowing anything about him."[33] What it is possible to know, of course, is a number of platitudes and clichés: here is "God's plenty," Chaucer "made" the English language, he is a master of psychology, and so on. These banalities are found in the book amid harangues against modern society, defenses of medievalism and Catholic virtues, and forays against various straw men, such as those (unnamed) scholars who have (somewhere) dared to assert that Chaucer was not a Catholic. Most maladroit is the attempt to prove Shakespeare an inferior artist when compared with Chaucer on the basis of the degeneration of the "true" democratic spirit of Chaucer's England to the insufferable Tudor-worship of Elizabethan England. Shakespeare's lush poetry and tragic vision are presumed to be presentiments of the anarchy and fragmentation of the modern world. The final effect of *Chaucer* is to sadden the reader at the sight of an excellent literary critic completely overwhelmed by the Catholic apologist.

## VII    *Chesterton and the Victorians*

For many Chestertonians, the supreme achievement of his career is the delightful little volume entitled *The Victorian Age in Literature* (1913). This work may be seen as one act in the lifelong drama which Chesterton played out in an attempt to understand, apologize for, and explain the great Victorians. No brief summary can completely delineate the breadth and depth of Chesterton's interest in the preceding century; one can only say that his interest has something of the qualities of a monomania. Thus the studies of Dickens, Shaw, and Stevenson are best viewed as a small part of a grand mosaic—

as a complex relationship between the Victorian Age and one of its heirs. That relationship was worked out in these studies of individual men, in *The Victorian Age in Literature,* and in countless essays about the Victorian literary figures and various facets of the nineteenth century.

Chesterton's admiration of the Victorians is evident in his candid admission that "I also was born a Victorian, and sympathize not a little with the serious Victorian spirit." On the death of Queen Victoria, he eulogized his sovereign with a lachrymose sentimentality worthy of a "navvy" on the docks. In one essay, Chesterton regrets the critical loss in his time of what he chooses to call the "great Gusto" of that age—referring to that love of life that he finds in Dickens. In another essay, he chastises that fashionable modern habit of "guying" the old Victorian virtues and taboos; he admired the long-lost arts of punctiliousness, popular music, and nonsense literature. He especially regrets the disappearance of the Victorian belief in the eternal verities.[34]

Like all the great Victorians, Chesterton is thoroughly Victorian in being anti-Victorian. He never could forgive the Victorians their materialistic spirit, their religious doubt, the failure of traditions, the enslavement of the common worker, and the triumph of ugliness. He admitted, however, that one could make little sense of an age of such contrasts and contradictions: "In short, when we look back on that time we see not a tide but an eddy, or a welter of eddies, in which each person is paddling his own canoe desperately in his own direction. . . . So far from simplifying itself with distance, it seems with distance to grow more dizzy and distracted. Wherever that age was drifting, it was to the place where we are now. And where in the world are we?"[35]

*The Victorian Age in Literature* is Chesterton's most detailed attempt to locate where he had been in order to know where he was. The basic thesis no longer seems remarkable: the Victorian age is best understood as a "compromise" between the rising forces of rationalism and the waning non-rationalistic forces (faith, belief, sentiment, emotion) of a preceding age, combining briefly into an unstable synthesis, and finally disintegrating. After a first chapter on the formation of this "compromise," the middle two chapters discuss the poets and novelists of the era, and a final chapter describes the "breakup of the compromise." The real pith of the book is a long series of sketches of the major writers—ones which predictably concentrate on their philosophies and their relationship to the central ideological struggle of their time between faith and secularism.

Completely unexpected and unique is the wit and lucidity with which Chesterton handles a subject too often wrapped in gloom and high seriousness. The pleasure which the book holds for any reader can only be displayed by some sample observations.

According to Chesterton, Matthew Arnold "kept a smile of heart-broken forbearance as of the teacher in an idiot school, that was enormously insulting." Tennyson "could not think up to the height of his towering style." As for the Christian Church and Victorian rationalism, "Neither was strong enough to expel the other; and Victorian England was in a state which some call liberty and some call lockjaw." The Oxford Movement was "a bow that broke when it had let loose the flashing arrow that was Newman." Utilitarianism is defined as "the philosophy in office, so to speak."

As always when discussing Chesterton, the strong temptation arises to continue quoting such gems. For many modern readers, especially those unfamiliar with the age or its writers, these are allusive, often gnomic; for others, they invest that period with new life. Naturally, there are Chesterton's usual lapses. Still unforgiven by the admirers of Thomas Hardy is Chesterton's judgment that the novelist was "a sort of village atheist brooding and blaspheming over the village idiot." And Chesterton is simply straining to create a *bon mot* when he speaks of Tennyson's work as "not a balance of truths, like the universe, [but] a balance of whims, like the British Constitution." Such excesses are easy to separate from the many riches in this volume, which remains one of the most pleasurable literary studies ever written.

## VIII    *Chesterton and Literature*

Chesterton's criticism may be described as an idiosyncratic blend of several critical approaches—moralistic, pragmatic, impressionistic, and judicial. It concerns itself with the *content* of the work of art, the moral and religious ideas particularly, because Chesterton recognizes the potential pragmatic effects art can have on an audience. Eschewing the deliberate, quasi-scientific approach of the academic critic, such criticism values the emotional effect of the moment and the personal response of the critic. It aims at some judgment of the work of art, whether it is "good" or "bad" and where it may be placed in comparison with other works. It is understandably at its best when the critic is at one with the artist, when, in Chesterton's case, the critic is treating such writers as Dickens and Browning.

What is absent in this summary is any mention of a *theory of art*, understandable, perhaps, because Chesterton is always uncomfortable in the role of theorist. He does have (as will appear later) a theory of imagination, but he rarely applies it to his practical criticism, and then in rather strange fashion: thus Browning and Stevenson are gifted with imagination, but not Blake or Shelley.[36] Other anomalies appear, as when he declares that history is "the greatest of all the works of the imagination," thus banishing to some cultural limbo the products of the composer, the painter, the sculptor, and the poet. In another essay Chesterton comes perilously close to Dr. Johnson by identifying imagination as "our own inside knowledge of mankind"; imagination viewed in this light is something like the collective wisdom of the human race, or what Pope called "what oft was thought but ne'er so well expressed."

A literary critic may operate without a theory of imagination, but he cannot function properly without some theory of words and their symbolic potential. Early in his career, in *G. F. Watts*, Chesterton had recognized the elusiveness of words, that every word communicates on more than one level, that each word is surrounded by a halo of personal and cultural connotations, many of these unconscious. In *Watts*, he scoffed at those modern Positivists who erroneously believe in the "modern dogma of the infallibility of human speech."[37]

The mood was short lived. For most of his life Chesterton demanded hard truths and clear values in what he read, and he assumed that the poet or novelist could provide them. (In his own poems and novels he is a purveyor of sharply defined ideas and clear characters, unencumbered, as we shall see, by

any ambiguities.) His basic view on language finds its clearest
expression in *Generally Speaking* (1928): "In the matter of
language, which is the main matter of literature, it is clear that
words are perpetually falling below themselves. They are ceasing
to say what they mean or to mean what they say; they are always
beginning to mean something that is not only quite different,
but much less definite and strong. And, in this fall of man's
chosen symbols, there may well be a symbol of his own fall.
He has a difficulty in ruling his tongue; not only in the sense
of the talking organ, but in the sense of the language he talks."[38]
Each word means something definite; the writer has only to
place his words in proper order to express his ideas in a manner
comprehensible to his readers. Chesterton is here asserting a
Positivism of language undreamed of by those he had criticized
in *Watts*.

Related to the problem of language is the more difficult
matter of symbolism. Chesterton defines symbolism as "not a
disguise but a display; the best expression of something that
cannot otherwise be expressed."[39] While he was willing to admit
that there is "something dark and irrational in human nature,"[40]
he refused to see the implications of such a view: that the
"something irrational" might never be capable of finding a
"rational" expression, or that the form that finally expresses it
will be equally dark and irrational. Chesterton's appreciation
of symbolism is really limited to what modern philosophers have
termed "signs," and, practically, to exercises in the reading of
allegory.[41]

Whenever Chesterton talks of "symbols," he is referring to
such "signs" as the Union Jack, the Cross, the longbow, the
postbox, home, a Trade Union badge—all of which he assumes,
incorrectly, have the same "meaning" and emotional content
for all men. Indeed, signs are a central prop of his philosophy:
"The most important things at the last are always said by signs,
even if, like the cross of St. Paul's, they are signs in heaven."[42]
It is a prescription for a uniformitarianism that ultimately
prevents the full appreciation of all poetry, but particularly
Romantic and modern poetry. Chesterton virtually shuts himself
off from a century and a half of English poetic accomplishment.

Chesterton's failure to understand the potentialities of the word does much to explain the numerous gaps in his practical criticism. He gives no articulated statement of artistic theory; he provides no sustained discussion of the problems of poetic communication; in fact, he has little to say about the English poets and what he does say is often disconcerting. "The poet," he says, is "the man who can express himself; the poet means the man who can make himself understood."[43] He is superior to other men in that he can "say exactly what he means, and that most men cannot."[44] The successful poets are those who work hardest at making themselves clear with the accepted meanings of words: Keats's "Ode to a Nightingale" is successful because "he went on pegging away until it made some sort of sense."[45] Blake, on the other hand, fails because "the actual words used mean one thing in Blake and another thing in the dictionary."[46]

As for modern poetry, it is beyond salvaging. The obscurity of the modern poets is "a defect of expression like a stammer"; the modern critics act criminally because they understand "what the artist wants to say and even save him the trouble of saying it."[47] Chesterton stands firmly with Dr. Johnson and the whole Augustan tradition in saying that good poetry is classical because the "perfectly classical can be understood by anybody."[48]

In short, the univocal approach to the problem of poetic communication is fatal in any literary critic, and it accounts for much of the current dissatisfaction with Chesterton. He was a transitional critic who was unwilling to take the step to a fuller understanding of the possibilities of symbolism. As part of his philosophy, he believed that the power of words must be held in check by some limitation on their meanings. One critic has explained Chesterton's "extraordinary fidelity" to the meaning of words as Thomistic; for St. Thomas, a word meant what it meant, words were indeed "refractions of the Word," and words could not be tampered with.[49]

Chesterton isolates himself entirely from the mainstream of modernism with this restricted view of words, as when he says "I am entirely on the side of the Puritan who thinks the symbol fictitious so long as he thinks the significance false."[50] The more modern view is to assume that a symbol is neither true nor false, but is exactly what the viewer (or reader) brings to it. One senses that Chesterton would have been happy, like his idol Dr. Johnson, compiling a dictionary and dictating the exact meanings to be applied to the words therein.

What is shocking is not that Chesterton spent his critical efforts knowing "what the artist is driving at," nor even that he should have been largely blind to the infinite beauties of poetry. The surprise is that this failure should have existed in a man like Chesterton whose religion was Catholicism of a particularly concrete type. What Chesterton found in Christianity was the power of incarnation, the redemption of earthly life from a meaningless and one-dimensional materialism. His undying message is the sanctity of worldly things, their magic and mystery, the divinity of all living things.

Yet Chesterton denies the power of the Logos, the creating word; his surface reading of poems, his tendency to message-hunt, his Positivistic theory of signs, commit him to a simplistic preoccupation with the thematic content of the works being criticized. The objects of the world are not prosaic for Chesterton, says Versfeld, but shine "with the exotic radiance of those fairy lands which are their port of origin." But such is not true about words; it is as though, having typed or dictated millions of words in the course of a lifetime, Chesterton found them vaporous, insubstantial, and unromantic.[51]

Perhaps the core of his problem is his belief in the simplicity of a divine universe, or at least its openness and availability to all men, even the ignorant; this egalitarianism in metaphysics, however well-intentioned, leads inevitably, however, to false ethics and falser esthetics. He would, for example, place restrictions on the full esthetic experience: "For my part, I should be inclined to suggest that the chief object of education should be to restore simplicity. If you like to put it so, the chief object of education is not to learn things; nay, the chief object of education is to unlearn things. . . . I would insist that people should have so much simplicity as would enable them to see things suddenly and to see things as they are."[52]

Such absolutism, whether in philosophy or esthetics, is no longer possible, if it ever was; modern man is disinherited from that Paradise in which Adam assigned one name to each thing. One of the disappointments of literary history is that, although

Chesterton was the leading spokesman of a sacramental view of the world, he would not permit the same sacramentalism to exist in literature. His criticism is always pulled beyond the unstable surface of the words that compose the book—diction, style, metaphor, and symbol—to the relative certainties if idea and character. His critical theory may be reduced to that complacent remark made by the hero of his *Tales of the Long Bow*, "What a fine thing is horse-sense, and how much finer really than the poetry of Pegasus!"[53]

This Benthamite attitude is the source of both his virtues and faults as a literary critic. No other writer of this century has been able to elucidate the central ideas of the major writers with such clarity and wit, or to place these ideas so clearly against the broader perspectives of their cultural background. Such gifts are not negligible ones, and a reader might do worse than to use Chesterton's essays as a first guide through English literature. While he may not find in them much subtlety or profundity, he will not lose himself in tangles of nuance, ambiguity, or academic jargon.

However, Chesterton's resistance to the magic lure of words and his pragmatic approach to literature make him an incomplete literary critic. Like Aristotle, Chesterton believed that the end of man is not a word but an act. This commitment to an ideal of man as a social and political animal explains why Chesterton's social criticism is more consistently satisfying than his work as literary critic.

CHAPTER 2

# Scouring the White Horse

THE image of Chesterton as a bibulous Pickwickian who faced the horrors of the world with the word "jolly" on his lips will not withstand the slightest inspection. His books easily confute this oversimplified picture and suggest that he was, as one critic says, "a displaced person, a letter delivered at the wrong address."[1] The address was the twentieth century into which Chesterton had been thrust complaining. He proudly confessed to being "medieval," an "unreasonable reactionary who refuses to face the great facts of the modern world."[2] The disclaimer does not mean that he was blind to reality, of course, nor did his aversion for modernity prevent him from launching an assault against his society that, in the scope of its vision and totality of its alienation, is equalled only by the work of Thomas Carlyle, John Ruskin, and William Morris—his predecessors in a noble strain of British literature.

Chesterton's criticism of his society is both practical and intellectual, socio-political and religious. To search for the initial impetus for his animosity or to assert, as some do, that he was essentially political, or to say that he was basically a fervid Christian who was angered by the mephitic religious atmosphere of his age—in short that everything he wrote was inspired by only one of these concerns—is futile.[3] The impressive feature of Chesterton's thought is its unity: as in the work of many of the great Victorians, his economic theory, religious faith, literary criticism, and political affiliations are inextricably woven together. One effect of this integration is that one may find important skirmishes of Chesterton's war with his culture in the most innocuous places—a lyric poem, an essay on cheese, or a short detective story.

This aspect of his work is symbolized by the title of one of his collections of essays: *Tremendous Trifles* (1909), a book

38

whose bitterness completely belies the innocence of its title. In it one discerns the main lines of his conflict with his society; the rest of the war may be observed especially in *Heretics* (1905); *All Things Considered* (1908); *What's Wrong With the World* (1910); *A Miscellany of Men* (1912); *Utopia of Usurers* (1917); *Fancies versus Fads* (1923); *William Cobbett* (1925); *The Outline of Sanity* (1926); *G.K.C. as M.C.* (1929); *The Well and the Shallows* (1935); *Avowals and Denials* (1938); *The End of the Armistice* (1940), and *The Common Man* (1950).

## I   Heretics

*Heretics* is important for a number of reasons, but particularly for its continuity with Chesterton's earlier literary studies; for *Heretics* picks up where the literary criticism leaves off. The working premise is boldly Chestertonian (and not unfamiliar): "the most practical and important thing about a man is still his view of the universe"(7); and so the distinguished authors of Chesterton's age should be treated "not personally or in a merely literary manner, but in relation to the real body of doctrine which they teach" (14-15). By summarizing and analyzing the philosophical views of his contemporaries, Chesterton implies that his own will be made clear.

What he finds in modern literature horrifies him. An army of heretics under the banner of the "negative spirit" (the spirit of pessimism inherited from the nineteenth century) are besieging modern man. The modern heretics are brilliantly equipped to see that the emperor has no clothes; however, they cannot tell him the magnitude of his loss or instruct him on the proper fashions he should adopt for the future. The modern reader finds in contemporary writing only skepticism or outright cynicism about moral and teleological values: "The human race, according to religion, fell once, and in falling gained the knowledge of good and of evil. Now we have fallen a second time, and only the knowledge of evil remains to us. A great silent collapse, an enormous unspoken disappointment, has in our time fallen on our Northern civilization" (24-25).

The modern inability to discover an absolute Good is the source of all heresies and confusion. This weakness, ironically, has not prevented modern writers from concluding that traditional religion and morality are "evil, stupidity, nonsense"; for, without any conception of Good, they still presume to define what Evil is. With equal sophistry, they are quick to place their faith in such panaceas as liberty, universal education, international brotherhood, and (especially) progress, implicitly attributing some "good" to them. Chesterton realizes, like Arnold before him, that these things are mere "machinery," means rather than ends; they inform man how he should travel but do not indicate any goal toward which individual lives or collective culture should be directed.

The ringmaster of the modern age is George Bernard Shaw, who once proclaimed, Chesterton bitingly remembers, "the golden rule is that there is no golden rule." Shaw's witty remark is, in Chesterton's view, a double-edged sword: one blade frees modern man, releases him from the bondage of ancient and outworn authority; but the other blade pins him into submission (55).

Thus modern heroism is best exemplified by Ibsen's Nora, who slams the door in *A Doll's House,* walks out into her brave new world, and leaves her husband and children behind. In each of the essays in *Heretics,* Chesterton pillories the writers who have destroyed the Bastilles of ancient authority or have figuratively permitted millions of Noras to leave their homes. Among the targets are Shaw's moral relativism and anti-idealism, which corrodes traditional morality; H. G. Wells's "scientism," which assumes the non-existence of the soul and the primacy of man's physical needs; modern Positivism and its destructive effect on myth, ritual, and religion; modern sociology, which advises men to accommodate themselves to the "trend" of the time, and thus escape the onus of moral responsibility; anthropologists, who cheapen Christianity by invidious comparisons with other religions; and the Whistler school of esthetics, which releases the artist from his traditional role as philosopher and priest (237-38).

All of this freedom comes at a price (11-14). After Nora has walked out the door, Ibsen cannot tell her where to go; all the signposts at the crossroads have been torn down in the riot of liberty which has run virtually unchecked since the Renaissance.

The eternity of becoming and the infinity of possibilities open to each man have turned out to be a treadmill to nowhere. Worse, such freedom has proven to be psychologically mischievous. The natural desire of the creature man is to have a goal, to have some definite purpose in life, and some authority in his society to help him reach his destination. Delivered from the bondage of older authorities, he immediately surrenders to some new master.

All of these modern philosophies conceal within themselves some new master, a new discipline, a harsher authority lacking the religious sanctification of the traditional authorities. Even Shaw's witticism denying the existence of a "golden rule" is an "iron rule" because it implicitly forbids certain rituals, actions, and beliefs. H. G. Wells's denial of a soul repudiates the possibility of a mysterious side to human experience. Walter Pater's exhortation to plunge into the sea of human emotion fails to warn man that these multitudinous passions can swallow him (104). By adjusting to "the tendency of the times," in obedience to the dictates of sociology, men have been transformed into "other-directed" automatons. And, freed by the anthropologists from witch doctors and the tyranny of priests, men are rapidly being ushered into new prisons hurriedly erected by the Commissars and Falangists of the new secular religions.

The central issue of *Heretics* is power, its sanctification, and its limitation. Indeed, power may be considered the one problem which unifies all the fields of Chesterton's activity. (One has observed, for example, Chesterton's fear of the unlimited power of words to mean anything one chooses them to mean.) In *Heretics*, he specifically attacks the modern delusion that the recently acquired gift of freedom—which was quickly translated into powers of self-realization and self-esteem—can and does expand endlessly outward. On the contrary, when the powers of individual and collective men are released, they are inevitably gathered in by some illegitimate authority, which then proceeds to misuse those powers. The power of the Catholic Church was overthrown by the Reformation, but the Protestant leaders then instituted even harsher controls to restrain their followers and prevent their own overthrow. Shaw cuts bonds, but then hypothesizes a future Superman toward whose realiza-

tion men must bend their agonized efforts (55-60). Whistler's
release of the ego results in his acting like a popinjay. After
destroying all the ancient icons, the new sciences—anthropology,
astronomy, geology—establish their own language and ritual;
and they also enthrone new deities to whom all men must
bend the knee.

The confusion over illegitimate power is also observable in
the social and political realms. Significantly, *Heretics* opens
with an essay on Rudyard Kipling and has a penultimate chapter
on the United States. In 1905, Chesterton was still critical of the
imperialistic adventures of the Boer War and of the Spanish-
American War. He viewed the United States as already display-
ing signs of advanced degeneracy, as had England, in that it
"fights small powers, but pretends that they are great powers,
in order to rekindle the ashes of its ancient emotion and
vanity" (267).

So easily did Chesterton's mind move from one level to another
that he is able to end his discussion of American imperialism
and close the book with an essay on "Slum Novelists and the
Slums." The seemingly heterogeneous material is always unified
by the underlying theme of misused power. In this last essay,
Chesterton denounces the system of government which gives
to the wealthy the power to make laws for the poor; the capitalist
system, which is legislation without representation, places "everything in the hands of a class of people who can always inflict
what they can never suffer" (278).

Chesterton's "Conclusion" attempts to provide a remedy for
this epidemic misuse of power, and particularly for that power
of intellectual expansiveness—what Cardinal Newman had called
"the immense energy of the aggressive intellect." For Chesterton,
as for Newman, the human mind is not structured to enjoy
unlimited freedom among an infinity of choices; it hungers for
stability, certainty, a resting place for its awesome powers. That
serene center may be found in the comforting arms of dogma:
"The vice of the modern notion of mental progress is that it is
always something concerned with the breaking of bonds, the
effacing of boundaries, the casting away of dogmas. But if there
be such a thing as mental growth, it must mean the growth

into more and more definite convictions, into more and more dogmas" (287).

The anodyne of dogma foreshadows the future conversion of Chesterton to the Catholic religion, a subject to be given attention later; for the present, the focus of interest of *Heretics* is not in its being a statement of philosophy or religion (although it is that), but in its being a development of the theme of power, the foundation of Chesterton's social and political criticism. As a book of philosophy, in fact, *Heretics* is singularly inept because it ignores the true "philosophers" of the age—Friedrich Nietzsche, Henri Bergson, and F. H. Bradley, for example. *Heretics* is not a philosopher's book but a journalist's; its author is interested in the forces then having an impact on the marketplace where common men gathered, and those forces in 1905 were Kipling, Pater, FitzGerald, and others already discussed.

In *Heretics*, Chesterton had stuck his finger on the place, like Goethe, and said, "Thou ailest here, and here." In most of the books that followed—in the years before and immediately after World War I—his critical eye is generally turned outward, its vision sharpened by the theme of *Heretics*. He could now more clearly discern the cruel and tyrannous arrangements of power evident in England and all over Europe. To this social, political, and economic criticism attention must now be given.

## II  *The Capitalist Tumor*

Chesterton's disaffection with the political and economic structure of modern capitalism is probably the most neglected facet of his thought. Perhaps his critics find it difficult to keep in focus the two images of the inflammatory revolutionist and the Pickwickian; or it may be that the irascibility in his political writings is as distasteful in an age of political alienation as the gushiness in his criticism. It would be, however, a serious distortion of any discussion of Chesterton to give only a cursory glance at his lifelong campaign to overthrow capitalism.

The core of his analysis of the capitalist evil is easily sketched in: capitalism had emerged along with the rising middle class at the end of the Middle Ages, it had perhaps served a real function at that time in contributing to the destruction of the feudal society, but it had rapidly degenerated into plutocracy.

The problem with capitalism is not trade, nor commerce, nor money, nor interest; the problem is power, and the fact that the power that wealth can buy has inexorably gravitated into the hands of a few men, who are able to tyrannize over their fellow citizens. In *The Well and the Shallows* (1935), one of Chesterton's last books, he says that "the cause of all the disasters of the modern world" is "the predominance of the trader."[4]

Nor is capitalism an eternal truth which was handed to Moses on Mount Sinai; it is, rather, a form of "Imperialism or Caesarism" peculiar to the modern era. It may be defined as "the dispossession of the populace of all forms of real productive property; all instruments of production in the hands of the few; all the millions merely the servants of the few, working for a wage, always an insecure wage, generally a mean and inhuman wage."[5] Far from providing a higher level of subsistence, as its defenders say, it keeps men "in wage dependence" and without capital. Its unbroken history of panics, strikes, and depressions proves that capitalism is most effective when operating with a high level of unemployment. Unemployment is a kind of "pivot upon which the whole process turns," which explains why any capitalist society is a Utopia for usurers.[6]

Leaning heavily on the arguments of Ruskin, Chesterton tirelessly stressed the heavy toll which capitalism takes of the individual and society. Esthetically, it has created the "unearthly ugliness" of our times; socially, by encouraging women into the labor market, it has created a "moral feud and a commercial competition between the sexes"; metaphysically, it has rendered modern life "insignificant."[7] Like Ruskin, Chesterton considers the division of labor the major source of modern evils, necessitating as it does "specialism"—specialization of the individual. The common man no longer dares to aspire to a wide range of interests and to a "universality" of spirit because he is intent on perfecting himself at a trade that will "uphold him in a more or less ruthless society."[8]

Factory workers are merely fragmented puppets who are manipulated hourly by the forces of the marketplace. Specialism is a malfunctioning of human powers because it is a "denial of the average"; the average common man is eliminated because certain individuals or classes are encouraged to monopolize the intellectual, emotional, or physical powers of the human race. The modern factory worker, for example, "gives up his head" when he goes to work because intellectual labor is not his life's work.[9] On a larger scale, one can see throughout society (except perhaps in the decaying aristocracy) a certain "blunting of the sentiment"—of the normal human sensibilities.[10]

The greatest irony of history, in Chesterton's view, is the synchronous appearance of a "free marketplace" and the power of repressive Puritanism: "The fact that bulks biggest in the modern industrial world is this: that its moral movements are much *more* utterly and ruthlessly repressive than the past forms of mysticism or fanaticism that commonly affected only the few."[11] The same point is made in *Heretics*: the so-called "emancipation" of modern man "has really been a new persecution of the common man." The persecution has been staged at the direction of the plutocrat, who has accumulated all the power and does not have to abide by the laws of the State; he is the only "emancipated" man, this "Uncommon man" who can be as eccentric, demented, or sadistic as he wishes because of his money.[12]

The end is in sight, for men will soon be marshalled "quite obviously to an enormous lunatic asylum." The theme of apocalypse reappears throughout the essays: Chesterton can see that society "is in the rapids"; or modern society is a maddening Walpurgisnacht from which man is trying to awake.[13] In *A Miscellany of Men*, Chesterton remarks that "These nations are really in danger of going off their heads *en masse*; of becoming one vast vision of imbecility, with toppling cities and crazy country-sides, all dotted with industrious lunatics. One of these countries is modern England."[14]

Chesterton also contended that the common man was haplessly trapped in a system which he did not make and wanted to see demolished. Tragically, his impotence is aggravated by the fraudulent and malevolent system of democracy that has been erected on top of the capitalist economy.

### III  *The No Difference System*

Influenced by his brother and Belloc, Chesterton decided quite early in life (and certainly by 1906) that England's Parliamentary system was half farce, half cruel deception. He was congenitally skeptical about man's institutions in any case; thus he was sure that if Socialism or Communism replaced capitalism, it would "make no difference to the clerk if his job became a part of a Government department tomorrow."[15] Parliament was certainly no tabernacle of democracy in an age when the voters had been blinded by their educational and economic prisons. Like Dickens, Chesterton had seen the "hollow and empty business" of election campaigns in provincial Eatanswills. The Victorian extensions of the franchise he interpreted as additional dissimulations by the plutocrats: they gulled the voters into believing they had some political power, but, in reality, they were reinforcing the traditional strongholds of power.[16] The movement for female suffrage was simply the latest in a series of capitalist ruses.

Parliament was not the grand institution it pretended to be, a reflection of popular sentiment and the legislative arm of the common man. Like Belloc and his brother in their *The Party System* (1911), Chesterton regarded it as another mode of farcical democracy and as "the most detested and most detestable of all our national institutions."[17] The continuing "vulgarisation of modern life" caused by capitalism is presided over by the most vulgar people—the politicians of the upper classes, who accomplish whatever is accomplished in the "Mother of Parliaments" "unofficially, casually, by conversations and cliques."[18] All their efforts are bent to serve the "two most powerful elements in the governing class"—the Capitalist, who makes money on the laws that are passed, and the "Social Reformer," who takes great pleasure in seeing something done, no matter what.[19]

Chesterton's displeasure is succinctly stated in a pamphlet "I Say a Democracy Means. . ." (1941), which lists the essential features of a true democracy. Again the crux is power: in a true democracy, the power flows upward from the people to the elected representatives; in the English system, the power flows downward from the Cabinet (significantly a non-elected body) to the backbenchers, thence to the manipulated and terrorized populace. The people acquiesce partly out of fear and conformity, and, in England, out of an essential decency and desire not to offend. The result of all this surrender and this conspiring is the complete negation of a democratic system.[20]

The real rulers of modern Britain are an army of petty functionaries, the mechanical men with seemingly unlimited authority to shape the nation as they think best. These faceless figures are examined at some length in the profoundly bitter book, *A Miscellany of Men* (1912). The ultimate irony in the present scene is that these factotums—government doctors, social scientists, social workers, eugenists—are not entirely certain of their own "sciences." "The inspector, the doctor, the police sergeant, the well-paid person who writes certificates and 'passes' this, that, or the other: this sort of man is being trusted with more authority, apparently because he is being doubted with more reason. . . . We are putting the official on the throne while he is still in the dock."[21] Thus one hears of a town doctor who sent a poor woman to an insane asylum because she could not keep her house clean and her children decently clothed.[22]

Chesterton's diagnosis of modern society and of England's political system eventually led him to a conspiratorial interpretation of modern history, one not a little tinged with anti-Semitism; for he saw various evil forces as being in a *conscious* alliance to destroy democracy and individuality. Thus in the early *All Things Considered* (1908), he echoed the theme of *Heretics* in asserting that England had an "occult government". "We have in this country all that has ever been alleged against the evil side of religion; the peculiar class with privileges; the sacred words that are unpronounceable; the important things known only to the few."[23] And he speaks elsewhere of the "powers and privileges" that are now beyond the reach of even the moderately rich and are "out of the power of everybody except a few millionaires."[24]

Other men have failed to see this conspiracy, of course, but only because most men find it difficult to "believe in such simplicity of scoundrelism."[25] Furthermore, the truth is neatly concealed by the newspapers, which are also a part of the plutocratic establishment. The conspiracy of power has everywhere shut out the light, and it increasingly threatens to murder freedom and humanity.

## IV   A View of History

The universal blindness to the capitalist conspiracy is, to
Chesterton, reinforced by another act of concealment: men have
been taught an erroneous version of history, one which modern
Englishmen "have absorbed from childhood." That myth is the
"Whig version of history," imbibed by generations of Englishman through a careful reading of Thomas Babington Macaulay's
essays, and his *History of England* and derivative works. The
myth teaches that the industrial world is the acme of human
achievement, that history is a record of unceasing progress,
that men have never been better off, but that things are certain
to get better. This myth of progressive history is the voice of
the industrialist against the farmer; the scientist and secularist
against the religious man; the future against the past.

Rejecting it in its entirety, Chesterton campaigned tirelessly
to convince his contemporaries that this new religion of "Progressive Evolution" was a lie.[26] His own instincts taught him that
numbers of societies had "relapsed into savagery" and would
continue to do so. He facetiously pointed to the advent of Prohibition in the United States as one example that showed how a
nation might fall "from better to baser drinks."[27] Indeed, one
might be hard pressed to prove that *any* progress had been
achieved in the history of man.

To counter the myth, Chesterton stated as early as 1913-14
in his *Daily News* articles that what was "much wanted" was a
"Working Man's History of England" which would act as an
antidote for the historical fantasies being dispensed by the
plutocracy.[28] Chesterton's emetic appeared as *A Short History
of England* in 1917, which perhaps accounts for its pervasive
anti-Prussianism and its somewhat muffled treatment of capitalism. Its main intent is to reverse at all points the Whig interpretation of English history.

The mere proportions of Chesterton's *History* give some sug-
gestion of the extent of the reevaluation: about two-thirds of
the space is given to the pre-1665 era (notably the Medieval
period), while all the accomplishments of science, technology,
and secular philosophies, as well as the growth of Imperial
Britain, are given only one-third. The Medieval period is clearly
Chesterton's "Golden Age," just as it was for Carlyle and Ruskin;

like them, and like other romanticizers of the Middle Ages during the Victorian period, Chesterton is willing to overlook the ugliness and brutality of that culture. The unattractive facts of the Medieval period are, to Chesterton, a small price to pay for its economic and social organization, which is the greatest that man has ever constructed; it protected the small farmer from the incursions of powerful landowners, it permitted peasants to own their own farms, it created guilds to protect the rights of tradesmen in the city, and it encouraged the practice of true democracy. Its final accomplishment was that it created an atmosphere in which fundamental human values were allowed to thrive.

The turning point in English history, to Chesterton, was the failure of Wat Tyler's revolution. For the first time in history, the king—who had traditionally derived his powers from the people—was prevailed upon by the nobles (rough equivalents of modern capitalists) to turn his power against the people. The king was alienated from the commons—the head from the body. In the vacuum of morality, the nobility leaped into a position of authority from which it has never descended. History repeated itself in the Reformation: Henry VIII was forced by his "Italianate" lords (a new class of capitalist squires) to deliver into their hands the vast spaces of rural England. (For those who resent the frequent intrusions of Chesterton's Catholicism, one may note that his discussion of Henry is mainly economic; the spoliation of the monasteries is barely mentioned.) Firmly established from the days of the Tudors is the precedent of the "new lawlessness of the rich" and a national policy of "plutocratic pillage."[29] The Reformation and Renaissance complete the destruction of the small farm and the guild; and even the Puritan rebellion is, to Chesterton, an "aristocratic" program of self-aggrandizement at the expense of King and Commons.

History repeats itself again in the not-so-glorious Whig Revolution. Led by the Hanoverian kings—"Teutonic rubbish"—the Whig landowners succeeded in destroying the last of the small farmers, depopulated the countryside, and turned the country toward a sanguinary "Industrial Revolution." In the Victorian period, England slipped further into atheism, jingoism, the concentration of wealth in the hands of the few, and the impoverishment and dehumanization of the many. The Reform Bills are frauds, postponements of democracy by such jugglers as Disraeli, "the brilliant adventurer" who remains forever the shining "symbol of the English aristocracy being no longer genuine" (266).

Chesterton's view of history is decidedly provocative, eccentric, exciting; it is open, however, to two serious objections. The lesser of the two, perhaps, is his uncompromising Francophilia, which attempts to conceal the long political and economic rivalry between the two Channel countries. Reading Chesterton's history, one would be unaware that historically, from William the Conqueror to Napoleon, the main external threat to England has been France.

A more serious objection to Chesterton's interpretation is his reluctance to recognize that political power had indeed shifted since the days of Queen Anne from the aristocrats to the new merchants and then increasingly to the lower classes. His blindness on this point is probably a result of his widespread disillusionment following the Liberal Party's victory in 1906; deceived by the presence on the front benches of scions of the best families in the nation, he was too quick to assume that nothing had changed. In addition, his feelings of personal futility and political impotence stemming from the Marconi trial contributed to a certain distorted perspective. Reading the *Short History of England,* however, one sees nothing of this; it is as though Victorian England had not confirmed the rise of the middle class, or as though the lower class had no political power at all. In spite of this eccentric and disproportionate "attempt to correct a disproportion" (220), Chesterton's history is a fascinating book whose transvaluation of terms is no mean accomplishment.

Chesterton gladly threw his anti-Whig version of history wherever such light was needed. The *Chaucer* volume, for example, emphasizes the "unity of the Middle Ages" to prove the degeneracy of modern times. Chaucer's pilgrims, one is told, knew where they were going because they had a single goal; increasingly, the modern problem is to "keep the company together" by finding a pilgrimage "on which they will ride together and remain different" (183). The last phrase is crucial. Arnold and Carlyle had praised the unity of the Middle Ages but had failed to realize the horrors possible under a modern technology which could convince, persuade, and organize the human masses into a "unity" of will-less robots. Chesterton perceived the dangers inherent in a culture which can manipulate and destroy the individual for the purposes of an ever-attractive but fallacious "unity." Chaucer's pilgrims had a single goal and purpose, but within the unity of their culture a maximum of individuality was condoned, as the *Canterbury Tales* only too clearly point out. In the modern era, there are "many forces making for a superficial sameness" while the last vestiges of Medieval individuality are being snuffed out (183).

Other essays show Chesterton attempting to discern where in history England had taken the wrong road. In some essays, his tragic figure is Mary Queen of Scots, who was destroyed by "new millionaires" like the Cecils and the Russells; her death marked the turn from the Renaissance (an age still penetrated with the Medieval religious outlook) to the Puritanism of Elizabeth. In other essays, the decline of England is identified with the introduction of the Hanovers; with George I, England meekly bowed to the capitalist yoke placed on it by the new merchant "princes." Wherever Chesterton places the blame—on the Crusaders at Hattin, on the executioners of Mary, on the regicides of the seventeenth century, on the cunning Disraeli—he sees only that Merry England is dead and its place has been taken by a modern wasteland.[30]

Chesterton willingly identified his own political allegiances with the Tory tradition of the eighteenth century—not, he hastily added, the "curious transitional type" represented by John Wilson Croker and William Gifford, but that of Swift, Pope, Bolingbroke, Goldsmith, and Johnson.[31] The word "Tory" grates on the ear when applied to Chesterton, who was officially a "Liberal" for much of his life and a "Radical" in his impulses. Anticipating a certain confusion among his readers, he defines the eighteenth-century Tories as "rebels." They were rebelling against "the oligarchy of the great Whig families, a very close corporation, indeed, having Parliament for its legal form, but the new wealth for its essential substance."[32] The Whig lords had acquired immense political power with their huge estates and then immediately set about harrying the populace with "evictions and enclosures, that its old common lands and yeoman freeholds might be added to the enormous estates." With these acts, the Whigs forever alienated themselves from the "ancient tradition of the English populace," which, one gathers, is a prerogative of the true Tory Party.[33]

Chesterton neglects to develop the similarities between the Tories and Whigs of the eighteenth century—failing to mention, for example, that it was Bolingbroke's Tory party which passed the Property Qualification Act (requiring a Member of Parliament to have an estate of at least 300 pounds annual value) and the Schism Act, which forbade all religious teaching except that of the Anglican Church. Nevertheless, it is extremely useful to see Chesterton framed within a long perspective of Tories back to Bolingbroke.

The Chestertonian view of English history finds its most poetic expression in a brief fantasy entitled *The End of the Roman Road* (1924). The narrator relates a dream in which he saw the road of British history leading from a coastal cathedral town to London. Suddenly the road is obstructed by a wall which surrounds "one of those estates that have made our modern history." Troops of heroes from England's past are seen marching—the Romans, the Normans, the Crusaders returning from the Holy Land, the members of the Medieval guilds, the rick-burners from the early industrial period. These groups are Chesterton's heroes; they are identified as bearers of the Mediterranean strain in English culture and the real pillars of England. They are contrasted with the "land-grabbers and usurers" who, like the owner of the estate, block the road. The dreamer achieves a vision of a final group of heroes, the British soldiers returning from the trenches of France, who are living proof that the English spirit is still alive. The dream ends ambiguously, however: a bridge into London beckons with promise, but the wall remains as a threat defying the men waiting on the road.

## V   William Cobbett

Appearing in the dream briefly is the figure of William Cobbett, perhaps Chesterton's favorite English writer (not excluding

Dickens) and certainly his model for social and political commentary. Cobbett's central role in Chesterton's version of English history is indicated by the volume *William Cobbett* (1925), a title which jostles uneasily with Chesterton's other books on the literature of the nineteenth century. Why, one asks, should Chesterton choose to write about this minor figure, this choleric politician and propagandist who seems to deserve his permanent resting place in the footnotes of history? Only by recognizing the centrality of social criticism in Chesterton's life can the reader understand why *William Cobbett* is perhaps Chesterton's most important piece of biographical criticism.

Within the first few pages of the book, one becomes aware that this is not a study of a literary figure but a panegyric on an early champion of "liberty, England, the family, the honour of the yeoman, and so forth."[34] In two respects—Chesterton's jaundiced view of industrial society and his reinterpretation of English history—Cobbett exactly parallels Chesterton, thereby providing him with a vindication of his fundamental articles of faith. His summary of Cobbett's role in English history provides the reader with an insight into the thought of both men:

What he saw was the perishing of the whole English power of self-support, the growth of cities that drain and dry up the countryside, the growth of dense dependent populations incapable of finding their own food, the toppling triumph of machines over men, the sprawling omnipotence of financiers over patriots, the herding of humanity in nomadic masses whose very homes are homeless, the terrible necessity of peace and the terrible probability of war, all the loading up of our little island like a sinking ship; the wealth that may mean famine and the culture that may mean despair; the bread of Midas and the sword of Damocles. In a word, he saw what we see, but he saw it when it was not there. And some cannot see it—even when it is there. (14)

To Chesterton, Cobbett's main gift was perspicacity, the vision to see the true nature of contemporary England which lay concealed from the myopic men around him. Because his clearsightedness enabled him to see the dangerous path England was taking, he was something of a poet-prophet, able to read the slightest clues and turn them into portents: that the English cathedrals were no longer attended, particularly in rural areas; that clusters of deserted cottages dotted the countryside; that the center of village social and political activity was the squire's mansion. For Cobbett, all of these signs were the skeletal parts of a morality play.

Cobbett's coevals were already being duped by "the veil which our version of history hangs between us and the real facts of our fathers." Rejecting the Whig version of history then just being formulated, Cobbett contrived to "turn all English history upside down," primarily by pointing out the evidences of the morality play (136). All of this means, of course, that Cobbett was doing for his age what Chesterton was to do a century later. Both were Tories, and both were incurably Radical; like Cobbett, Chesterton had an intuitive insight that permitted him to read implications into the transitory signs of the times; the essays of Chesterton may be read as counterparts of Cobbett's *Rural Rides*, consisting as they do of descriptions and prophetic warnings.

Like Cobbett, also, Chesterton was to be a failure; both men were unable to stunt the gigantism of modern life, or to halt the depopulation of rural England, the ugly urbanization, the growing influence of science and secularism. Yet Cobbett's presence (even in the footnotes of history) was reassuring evidence to Chesterton that his own reading of history and society was not a delusion and that there was a continuing strain of sanity in England which might eventually win through.

## VI  *Three Nations*

Chesterton's analysis of the illness of his own country did not take place in a vacuum but was, to a large measure, dependent on his awareness of how international relations affected the quality of life in England. Chesterton, we have seen, had spoken of modern nations "going off their heads en masse; of becoming one vast vision of imbecility."[35] One of these nations was his native England, but the disease of capitalism was most clearly pronounced in what one might call three nations: the United States, Germany, and Zion. England's own health would be improved immeasurably if she would be less imitative of these foreign models of industrial civilization. After making two personally rewarding trips to the United States—after each of which he duly performed the ritual of a book, *What I Saw in America* (1922) and *Sidelights on New London and Newer York* (1932)— Chesterton concluded that, while he loved America and Americans, he detested "Americanization." By this, he meant the combination of bigness, plutocracy, and industralization which tragically ensued after the defeat of the South in the Civil War.[36] For the present, England and other European nations were seemingly being forced by the limitless power of America's "economic pressure" to cast aside their own traditions and to accept the ideal of plutocratic capitalism from across the Atlantic. In a speech printed as *Culture and the Coming Peril* (1927), Chesterton concluded that America's "enormous scale" and "insensibility to the idea of size" were the most dangerous elements on the international scene. Logically, he therefore viewed the collapse of the stock market in 1929 and the Depression of the 1930's with something approaching religious ecstasy.

Chesterton's love-hate relationship with the United States was almost genteel in comparison with the violent aversion he felt toward Germany. This dislike derived naturally enough from Chesterton's classical education, his friendship with Belloc, his Catholicism, and the death of Cecil Chesterton in the Great War. Chesterton turned his prejudices to account during the war by venting his wrath in the essays collected as *The Barburism of Berlin* (1914) and *The Crimes of England* (1915), which displayed the same Francophilia as *A Short History of England*. The crimes perpetrated by England were all those turning points in history when England betrayed her Franco-Mediterranean origins and aligned herself with Protestant Prussia. The blackest deed of all, of course, was the importation of the Hanoverians, which doomed "merrie olde England" by giving the seal of approval to Whig capitalism.

Chesterton's blatantly propagandistic productions are less important than the constant strain of Germanophobia running throughout his works, manifesting itself in his villainous Prussian professors and in his acid comments about German culture and politics. Frequently, he equates "industrialism" with "Prussianism," and then defines the latter word as "science combined with organization."[37] To Chesterton's credit, one may add finally that his predictions about the course of history were remarkably accurate. During the 1920's and 1930's he pointed to the numerous errors perpetrated at Versailles, warned against the rise of a re-armed Germany, and argued against any diplomatic encouragement of a strong German state. In *The End of the Armistice* (essays of the 1930's published in 1940), he sketched the future with uncanny prescience: that the élite German General Staff would rise again, that England would sleep, that Poland would be the first prize, that the conflict would be worldwide and more horrible than anything yet seen on the face of the earth.[38] In his distrust of the Germans, Chesterton has been thoroughly vindicated.

Less praiseworthy was the continuing strand of anti-Semitism in Chesterton's works, one that paradoxically lies side-by-side with his deeply felt Christian humanism that affirmed that all men are "sacred beings of equal value in the sight of God."[39] Like Belloc—or Hitler, for that matter—Chesterton felt that his nation's health was being eroded from within by the forces of Jewish villainy, the intellectuals, the merchants, and the financiers dear to legend. Partly a religious prejudice (resting on the so-called facts of the Crucifixion) and partly nationalistic, such anti-Semitism traces the decline of England from Cobbett's day, when there was a misguided "handing over of England to the wealthier Jews."[40]

Chesterton's answer to the Jewish problem was Lord Balfour's: the resettlement of the Jewish people in Palestine. In *The New Jerusalem* (1922), another travel book that pounded at a point, he argued for Zionism with some authority and originality. His main argument was that, because modern Jews were expatriates, they had no natural loyalty to the states in which they found themselves; in fact, because they have family ties with other countries (the Rothschilds come to mind), their presence elsewhere is an invitation to civil disobedience and treachery. The confused network of loyalties, to family and to nation, meant that the modern Jew could not be trusted to be a dutiful citizen. "The thing that is really vulgar, the thing that is really vile, is to live in a good place without living its life."[41] Presumably, the fact that Disraeli had had an Anglican upbringing and followed that faith, had served as a member and leader of his government, and had eventually been ennobled by his Queen counted for nothing.

The resettlement program outlined in *The New Jerusalem* was to aim for "as few Jews as possible in other established nations." If total resettlement in Zion were impossible, then steps toward identification (yellow stars of David?) and segregation "in some sort of self-governing enclave" were recommended. One reads with horrible anticipation of a "final solution." It does no good to hear Chesterton say that some of his friends are Jews,[42] to excuse Chesterton by saying that such anti-Semitism was the intellectual freight of most educated men of his time, or to hear Chesterton say (in *The End of the Armistice*, on the subject of an early Nazi pogrom) "I am certainly not enough of an Anti-Semite to say that it served them right." The odor of Auschwitz and Belsen do much to mock, to impeach, Chesterton's innocent formulae for Medieval Catholicism, peasant proprietorship, and Little England.


## VII  *Aux Barricades*

When one reads Chesterton's statement that "For a hundred years after Cobbett's forlorn hope we are confronted again by Cobbett's question  We must go back to freedom or forward to slavery,"[43] one should have no doubt about Chesterton's apocalyptic vision: men have reached the moment for revolution. The foremost defender of the patriotic habit of mind, the lover of old England, perhaps the one man who most unrelentingly defended the traditions of the past, was a radical aiming for the complete overthrow of his society. His revolutionary activism is as strident and emotional as anything heard in Barcelona, St. Petersburg, or Rome during his turbulent lifetime. The traditional image of Chesterton bent over a book and a tankard at some pub must be supplemented, therefore, with the image of a huge man with arm upraised and a clenched fist.

Like most revolutionary theorists, Chesterton's hope lies in the common people, particularly in the timeless love for and attachment to the land of the English people. England will survive, will undoubtedly rise from its ashes, because of the

tradition of Christmas that persists "through the madness of
Calvinism, the grossness of Industrialism, and the deepening
darkness of Social Reform."[44] Let no one suppose, however, that
the English people, once awakened, will be merciful: "If we
wake out of this throttled, gaping, and wordless nightmare, we
must awake with a yell. The Revolution that releases England
from the fixed falsity of its present position will be not less noisy
than other revolutions. It will contain, I fear, a great deal of that
accomplishment described among little boys as 'calling names';
but that will not matter much so long as they are the right
names."[45]

The revolution is against the forces of darkness; it is Armageddon, apocalypse, the overthrow of Ahriman. It is not the
Marxist Revolution (an overthrow in which "good things shall
perish also") but a movement "backward to freedom," to some
religious, pre-capitalistic past. In *What's Wrong With the World*
(1910), one is told that one must "repent and return; the only
step forward is the step backward."[46] Whoever has the same
dream of revolution and humanity—his friends on the *New
Witness*, Syndicalists, Guild Socialists—are invited to participate
in this "rolling back" to some distant golden age.[47]

The problem is not how one initiates the revolution; Chesterton is convinced that there is a reservoir of good will in the
world, that most men can be made to see that their present state
is terrible, and that the gospel of "progressive evolution" is a
lie. The major problem—and the main effort of Chesterton's
journalism—was to convince men that they are headed in the
wrong direction and that there are practical alternatives to their
present plight. That alternative—a shrine toward which a modern pilgrimage must direct itself—is "Distributism." This is
a word that is now only a dim memory, but it was for most of his
life the center of Chesterton's work and preoccupation.

# CHAPTER 3

# Three Acres and a Cow

IN the middle of G. F. Watts Chesterton had decried "the ruling element in modern life, in all life, this blind and asinine appetite for mere power. There is a spirit abroad among the nations of the earth which drives men incessantly on to destroy what they cannot understand and to capture what they cannot enjoy" (110). Chesterton's analysis, one now can see, was remarkably perceptive. Other men would require the disaster of World War I to strip bare the sordid realities of modern technocratic society. Only then could they discern that the Victorian calm was as fragile as the supposedly unsinkable Titanic.

In retrospect, what followed the Great War was an efflorescence of political experiments extending from Japan to Spain, and beyond. The Soviet revolution—that surprising fulfillment of Karl Marx's dreams on the steppes of Russia—seems now to be only one of the exotic plants growing in the ashes of World War I. We can clearly perceive that almost every industrialized nation in the world had some flirtation with one or more strange political programs. On the left there were the spread of Socialism in England, the appeal of Communism in the United States, and numerous Socialist-colored regimes in Europe; on the right, there were the militarism of Japan, the Fascism of Spain and Italy, and the National Socialism of Germany. The air was filled with the voices of political and economic quacks, each of them armed with a nostrum as likely to kill as to cure the patient.

So certain was Chesterton of such danger that much of his writing is directed at refuting these new and insidious panaceas. In fact, his work shows a curious double focus; he attacks simultaneously the established capitalist society and the enemies trying to destroy it. This ambivalence may be seen in the essay in G.K.C. as M.C. in which he laments that "the public powers or new proposals are breaking up the old rural life of England; they have already broken it up."[1] Generally, he was speaking of the "new proposals" of the political left; for he considered them more threatening than those from the right.

## I  *Fascism and* The Resurrection of Rome

Traveling to Italy in 1929, Chesterton had been frankly attracted to the operation of Mussolini's Fascism, perhaps because Mussolini—realizing the importance of this Catholic journalist from England—had granted him a private interview. Chesterton recorded his reactions to the dictator and his new nation in a book with the pregnant title, *The Resurrection of Rome* (1930). Hindsight permits one to discern the naïveté of the main argument; for once, Chesterton's usually penetrating eye had been dimmed by the spell of Italy, Rome, the Catholic-Mediterranean culture.[2] Mussolini, he concluded, was a serious, well-intentioned, sympathetic leader of a great people. The old bromide about the trains running on time is dutifully mentioned; and, while it may be conceded that *Il Duce* is occasionally theatrical and that the Italian people are somewhat given to gaudy pageantry, the English journalist thinks these peccadillos are inherent in the Latin peoples.

Chesterton regrets that Mussolini had to step over a mountain of corpses to obtain power, but one must break eggs to make an omelet; all revolutions, including Italy's Fascist revolution, are "stained by many infamous crimes and infamous acts of violence."[3] Furthermore, the end justifies the means (a shocking argument from Chesterton): Fascism has succeeded in controlling the capitalists. The Fascist government is unique in that it has isolated itself from the malign influence of the financial centers of power. The journalists of the world and the English liberals bleat piteously about the limitations on speech and the franchise in the Italian system; but, queries Chesterton, what are these compared to the hypocrisies of capitalism? How can there be free speech in Britain where the press is owned by the plutocrats? Does the vote mean anything in a country where the major parties compose a "No-difference system"? The brutalities of Fascism are at least open for all to see; the capitalist system conceals its inequities and horrors (particularly the fact that "Wealth buys power") behind pleasant words.

Italian Fascism as Chesterton observed it in 1929 resembled his own schema for political reformation. Part of its appeal to him resided in its alliance with official Catholicism; for, when he was faced with the Protestant version of Fascism in Germany, his reaction was distinctly cool. For example, in *The Resurrection of Rome*, he argues that Mussolini was instilling in his people a sense of discipline that was warm and humanistic in comparison with the "heavy regimentation which pedants in 'scientific' states would impose on herds"—an unmistakable allusion to Prussia. Also, he asserts but does not prove that the discipline in Italy is healthier because it is a "popular appetite and a popular pleasure" (224-25).

As the 1930's advanced, Chesterton's defense of Italian Fascism was increasingly enfiladed by the dire effects arising from the triumph of Naziism. He continued to defend Fascism in general as no more totalitarian than capitalist England—by ignoring the plain facts before him. At other times, he dismissed National Socialism as a "parody" of Fascism, "a new and naked nationalism" that had substituted itself—like a cuckoo egg in another bird's nest—for the old, religiously founded nationalism.[4] In 1934, near the end of Chesterton's life, he swallowed his Germanophobia sufficiently to defend all Fascism as "in some ways a healthy reaction against the irresponsible treason of corrupt politics."[5] In the next year, he was willing to admit, however, that Italy was one of the "tyrannies" in Europe but that it "had not in fact torn up certain traditions of popular freedom in Catholic countries, which have been, and are being, more and more ruthlessly and rapidly torn up and uprooted in Protestant countries."[6] The division in Chesterton's mind was still along religious lines.

## II  *The Threat from the Left*

Much stronger in the post war years was the appeal of Socialism and Communism to the peoples of Europe. Chesterton was frank in admitting that he had once been a Socialist (before the turn of the century, as had many of his class); and even today it is difficult to untangle his economic and political goals from the programs, say, of such Socialists as George Bernard Shaw. Chesterton calmly predicted that Communism was the wave of the future, but he found this no reason for being apoplectic (as were the plutocrats in their Pall Mall clubs) or violent (as were the "Bolshie-hunters" in the 1920's in the United States).

Chesterton soothed his readers with the thought that Communism, when it came, could be no worse than capitalism and was probably to be preferred to it. Some critics have rightly pointed out that Chesterton "never quite grasped the significance of the Russian Revolution,"[7] but then he himself felt that no one had ever grasped the significance of capitalism. In one of the last Father Brown stories, the priest-detective says:

Of course, Communism is a heresy; but it isn't a heresy that you people take for granted. It is Capitalism that you take for granted; or rather the vices of Capitalism disguised as a dead Darwinism. Do you recall what you were all saying in the Common Room, about life being only a scramble, and nature demanding the survival of the fittest, and how it doesn't matter whether the poor are paid justly or not? Why *that* is the heresy that you have grown accustomed to, my friends; and it's every bit as much a heresy as Communism. That's the anti-Christian morality or immorality that you take quite naturally.[8]

According to Chesterton, the Marxists have been too lenient, too honorable in calling outright villains "capitalists" when they deserve to be called "cads"—and worse.[9] This Marxist generosity is, to Chesterton, an important clue to the fact that capitalism and Communism are twin systems, resting as they do on the same idea—the centralization of wealth and, its corollary, the abolition of private property. It is immaterial that they differ on where they wish to centralize the wealth—Communism in the state, and capitalism in the hands of the most powerful plutocrats; both succeed in crushing the small individual by taking his property from him.[10]

While he found Communism's concern for the welfare of men a laudable impulse, Chesterton was never able to embrace Marxism, based as it is on the double-pronged theory of materialism and determinism. From his religious standpoint, man cannot be determined at all, and least of all by any economic parameters. Chesterton viewed Marxist theory as "Bolshevik bosh" rooted firmly in the Victorian materialism of which Karl Marx was such a prominent product himself. Armed with the "economic and biological determinism" of their Victorian forbears, the Marxists were noisily parading across Chesterton's field of vision with "second-hand goods and third-rate theories."[11]

The unrecognized horror of the period rested in the fact that, even if not Communist, men were already dwelling in what Belloc pungently called "The Servile State," which was to be more fully delineated by Aldous Huxley's *Brave New World* (1932) and George Orwell's *1984* (1948). Capitalism may be defined, says Chesterton, as a dehumanizing "proletarianism";[12] for the wealthy few manipulate the laborers in a vast slave camp and are abetted by an ever-expanding government. The government invades the privacy of its citizens much as religion once did; the instrument of this invasion is the telephone, which symbolizes the individual's subjection to some central power. Capitalism has, therefore, dressed itself in all the trappings of modern totalitarianism; and it has succeeded in sacrificing liberty without providing the equality it has promised or the standard of living it supposedly guarantees. In *Sidelights on New London and Newer York* (1932), Chesterton ruefully warns against the tragedy lying in wait: "Under the Servile State the soul will be yet more horribly free. There will be nothing to prevent a man losing his soul, as long as he does not lose his time or his ticket or his place in the bread queue. We need not be surprised, therefore, if the laborious organization and combination of our time encircles a singular loneliness" (195-96).

At this point, it is hard to resist showing how Chesterton could marshall his literary gifts for the purposes of social criticism—a trick which he had learned from Ruskin and Arnold. In *Eugenics and other Evils* (1922)—a book which convincingly reveals the collectivist tendencies of capitalism—he analyzes a popular music-hall song, one verse of which reads:

> Father's got the sack from the water-works
> For smoking of his old cherry-briar;

Father's got the sack from the water-works
'Cos he might set the water-works on fire.

A touchstone for understanding collectivism, the song centers
on the conflict between the individual citizen and the anonymous
organization; the hero is the father, the main prop of the family,
and the common laborer; the cherry-briar pipe is the simple
pleasure of the common man's life, which the organization
resents because it undermines efficiency; and, says Chesterton,
it is the one small detail of the individual's life which the
organization cannot control; the pipe signifies old habits, old
ways of thinking, the personal element that must be rooted out.
Failing to do so, the organization must ostracize the individual
human being as a potential threat.[13]

Communism is the wave of the future because the West has
been prepared for it: collectivism, anonymity, centralization are
already a way of life. Ready to act as functionaries of the
Communist state are the commercial men, the bankers, the
plutocrats who have already presided over the collectivist
schemes of Manchester and Wall Street.[14] Before the final step
is taken, Chesterton's task was to publicize other alternatives
to capitalism or Communism. Thus in 1912, in the very angry
*A Miscellany of Men,* he writes: "It is quite unnecessary to
say that I should prefer Socialism to the present state of things.
I should prefer anarchism to the present state of things. But
it is simply not the fact that Collectivism is the only other
scheme for a more equal order.... We might have peasant
proprietorship; we might have the compromise of Henry George;
we might have a number of tiny communes; we might have
cooperation; we might have Anarchist Communism; we might
have a hundred things" (43-44). The social critic had to lead
his readers out of polarized ways of thinking that serve only
to preserve this "present social madhouse."

### III   *Distributism*

In an essay on "Elegy Written in a Country Churchyard,"
Chesterton claims that the description in which the ploughman
and his cattle disappear into the darkness gives one a "perspective of vanishing things," for the rural setting is soon

destroyed and the ploughman returns as "either a scientific works manager or an entirely new kind of agrarian citizen."[15] There is much of Gray's *persona* in Chesterton, a figure sitting in a cemetery at dusk, lamenting the loss of all old things but especially the disappearance of rural England. Lost in his thoughts, Chesterton ignored the harangues of the Imperialists, who were still convinced that England could "grow as rich as America was"; he could equally shut out the promises of Fascists, Communists, and Fabians. The problem of power and the limitations on power could not be solved by economic theory alone; the solution had to take into account a number of religious, social, and psychological factors.

Chesterton found his answer to the problem of gigantic accumulation of wealth and the amoral exploitation of political power in the institution of private property. There were others, of course, who were advising that the monopolies and trusts be broken up; but it is difficult to find anyone else for whom private property, the wide distribution of property, was such a central article of belief. Private property is the fundamental underlying concept of Chesterton's political and economic thought, and to overlook it, to dismiss it as visionary rubbish, is to miss a major focus of his writing. To say that he wrote only one book on "Distributism" (*An Outline of Sanity*) is also erroneous. It is more accurate to say that he never missed an opportunity to inject Distributist ideas into his essays and poems. Furthermore, there is general agreement that he shortened his life by his Herculean labors on three periodicals expressly designed to propagandize Distributist ideals: *The Eye Witness* (1911-12), *The New Witness* (1912-23), and *G.K.'s Weekly* (1925-26). And how can one measure the cost in time and energy of numerous speeches, debates, and meetings for the benefit of the Distributist cause?

It is axiomatic with Chesterton that capitalism, "the unbalanced race after private profit," had ended with an imbalance of political power.[16] Socialism provided no remedy because it simply completed "the Capitalist concentration"; it took private property from its owners and turned it over to an equally anonymous state.[17] Socialism and capitalism are psychological failures, in that the human mind cannot comprehend, criticize,

or love human organizations on such a vast scale. The tendency
of the times must be reversed; men must move backward from
more complete concentrations of property to a redistribution of
property to large numbers of people. The psychological gain
would be a return to a scale of life that the individual could
see and comprehend; the social gain would be a rebalancing
of powers among numerous men. Behind both of these ideas
was the religious truth, the "mature mystery of private property,"
which cannot be understood but must be accepted mystically.[18]

The program has the unfortunate name "Distributism"—only
a slight improvement over what it was called at first, "Dis-
tributivism." Its roots may be traced to Belloc and Cecil Chesterton's *The Party System,* which advocated a return to medievalism
—and even more to Pope Leo's encyclical *Rerum Novarum*
(1891), which established man's natural right to own property
and encouraged the widest possible distribution of property.
The psychological basis was emphasized: Chesterton was always
ready to argue that the wish to own private property proved
that Distributism was a "human" system, while other economic
programs were dehumanized and "abstract."[19] One senses something "neoclassical" in the assertion that Distributism "is so sane
and simple, so much in acordance with the ancient and general
instincts of men."[20] (One wonders, however, why, if the desire
for property is instinctual in man, the concentration of property
in a few hands has accelerated in recent centuries.)

The Distributist program is described in detail in *The Outline
of Sanity* (1926) and *Avowals and Denials* (1934). The latter
book admits that "reversing, or even resisting, the modern
tendency to monopoly or the concentration of capital" (151)
would be difficult because of the vast political power already
invested in the hands of the few, but *The Outline of Sanity*
unrelentingly shows how a reduction of capitalist power may
be effected: "We do not offer perfection; what we offer is
proportion. We wish to correct the proportions of the modern
state; but proportion is between varied things.... We do *not*
propose that in a healthy society all land should be held in
the same way; or that all property should be owned on the
same conditions; or that all citizens should have the same
relation to the city. It is our whole point that the central

power needs lesser powers to balance and check it, and that these must be of many kinds: some individual, some communal, some official, and so on" (56).

This balancing of powers, in effect, moves in the direction of ruralization, thereby placing Chesterton in the line of the great nineteenth-century Romantic primitivists, extending backward through Morris and Tolstoy, to Wordsworth, to Cowper, Goldsmith's "Sweet Auburn," and ultimately to the small agricultural city-states of ancient Greece. To Chesterton, the tragedy of Europe and modern England was the great migration into the cities, a turmoil into which millions of peasant-citizens had disappeared with all their arts and crafts. The remedy proposed by Chesterton is the re-creation of this body of yeomen, and their resettlement on the land after equipping them with traditional skills and knowledge of handicrafts.

*The Outline of Sanity* argues that Distributism is not just a castle in the air but has an urgent practical significance. Chesterton thought that the present concentration of specialized laborers in large industrial cities was inviting economic and social disaster. In a time of stress, such specialists would find themselves helpless, whereas the Distributist system would provide "in the community a sort of core not only of simplicity but of completeness . . . a type that was truly independent; in the sense of producing and consuming within its own social circle" (136). Following the Wordsworthian clue that an individual is psychically stronger when "nearest to his natural origins," Chesterton was certain that his ideal citizens would escape the domination of "despots and demagogues" (133).

Beneath these reasoned arguments is an article of faith: that there is a "very large element still in England that would like to return to this simpler sort of England . . . to the roots of things, where things are made directly out of nature" (123). Although the English countryside cannot support all the people—a point Chesterton grants—the task of bringing about a mass movement to the country does not arise (187, 57). The more troublesome problem is to "stop the other people from doing what they are doing now" (56). One may begin by asking for volunteers at first (such as those who settled the virgin lands of Siberia in the 1930's)—those who liked raising chickens and vegetables in their small, urban backyards. Others would follow as the program feeds on its early successes.

To the cynic who asks how city people may be transformed into successful farmers, Chesterton cleverly answers: "If human nature has been hopelessly changed and fixed by less than a hundred years of industrial life, why was it not already hopelessly fixed by hundreds and thousands of years of rural life."[21] Education is the practical answer, once one has found the volunteer farmers and landlords willing to sell their land cheaply. It is above all "vital to create the experience of small property, the psychology of small property, the sort of man who is a small proprietor."[22]

One detects that most of this education rests on the principle of sink-or-swim. Chesterton trusts that the English city-dweller, faced with the problem of operating "three acres and a cow," will somehow muddle through by using his native wits. One may note in passing that a central point in the Distributist League doctrine was the "maximum initiative on the part of the citizen."[23] Given the facts of man's free will and the native cleverness of John Bull, Chesterton argues in *The Outline of Sanity,* the peasant will prove to be a jack-of-all-trades "who almost always runs two or three sideshows and lives on a variety of crafts and expedients. The village shopkeeper will shave travellers and stuff weasels and grow cabbages and do half a dozen things, keeping a sort of balance in his life like the balance of sanity in the soul" (179). One may cynically inquire how such talents could have sparkled in Ireland in the 1840's or in the American Dust Bowl in the 1930's. Chesterton's rural idyl is, ironically, a restatement of Darwin's "survival of the fittest," and seems hardly as humane as it claims to be.

In the city, Distributism will be enthroned by the force of good will. Enlightened by the new gospel, the common people will support only the small shops and boycott the large stores and businesses into submission. One surmises that these ordinary citizens would resist the lure of lower prices held out by the large emporiums (recognizing the evil motives behind such lures) and patronize the small shops out of good will. Meanwhile, "little laws" and the "more sweeping operation of larger laws" (96) would encourage the diffusion of wealth. Some of the legal innovations Chesterton sketches are profit-sharing in small shops, management of larger businesses by guilds of co-owners, free legal aid for the poor, heavy taxes on real-estate transactions involving the transmission of land from small property-owners to large, elimination of primogeniture, and subsidies for "certain experiments in small property" (79-80). Contending that *The Outline of Sanity* is not the forum for details, but only a "sketch of first principles," its author then moves on to larger problems.

Faced with the problem of machine-ownership, that incubus of all Utopia-builders, Chesterton takes an ambiguous position somewhere between Edward Bellamy (who apotheosized the humane use of machine culture in his *Looking Backward,* 1888) and William Morris (whose rustic Utopia in *News from Nowhere,* 1890, required the smashing of all machines). In the abstract, Chesterton argues that if machinery is indeed a curse, why retain it? "There is no reason why we should not leave all its powers unused, if we have really come to the conclusion that the powers do us harm" (145). Since we are not yet certain on this point, however, one may experiment with a system whereby local guilds can own shares in and derive profits from large machine equipment. This plan is a temporary expedient— "a practical programme that could be a preliminary to a possible spiritual revolution of a much wider sort" (148). Chesterton seems to be looking into Cobbett's crystal ball and envisaging an eventual Luddite rebellion in which the mechanical ricks will again be demolished to preserve man's spiritual health.

## IV *Distributism in Practice*

Fearing a charge of sickly fantasizing, Chesterton endeavors periodically to give his Distributist dream a local habitation and a name. A recurrent example in his works is the Medieval guild, which he claimed successfully checked the expansionist competitive forces of the Renaissance.[24] The Middle Ages is one example of the Distributist ideal, the age when "ethics and jurisprudence affirmed the principle of private property";[25] if that age seems exotic to modern men, it is only because they calmly tolerate practices which Medieval men punished severely—

usury, monopoly, interest, speculation. To Chesterton, the last
remnant of the guild idea in modern times is the medical
profession, which requires high standards from its members
and thwarts the concentration of power in the hands of the
few by forbidding "certain expedients of self-assertion or self-
advertisement." Again the aggrandizement of power is the
thing to be avoided.

Chesterton's prototypes of Distributism on a national scale
were to be found in such modern countries as France, Ireland,
Montenegro, Serbia, and, later, Nazi Germany. During World
War I, Chesterton eulogized Montenegro as "almost as much
in advance of England as it is of Germany" because its people
have land.[26] In defiance of the testimony of a number of French
novelists, Chesterton similarly praised France and French provincial life as idyllic; and he hailed the courage of the French
settlers who bore the seeds of Distributism into the wilds of
Canada. Shortly before his death, he claimed to see "the increasing influence of the Distributist State" in Hitler's theory
of the Nation.[27]

His paradigm for Distributism is modern Catholic Ireland,
which perfectly integrates the coequal elements of a sane
religion and a vigorous peasantry. Again, disregarding the testimony of recent history, Chesterton proclaims that the "present
prosperity of the Catholic peasantry" proves that Ireland has
"before our very eyes turned a sudden corner and stepped into
a place in the sun."[28] In *Irish Impressions* (1919), which first
appeared in the *New Witness* (1918), Chesterton attempts to
vindicate Ireland's controversial role in the war. The main thesis
is that Ireland has achieved a remarkable stability that sets it
off from modern Europe. By discouraging any significant degree
of industrialization, Ireland has protected its peasantry and now
closely approximates the Greek *polis*. Ireland has failed only
where she has flirted with capitalist modernism, where she has
allowed the family farm to be bought by absentee landlords,
and where the farm has been used only to make money.

Ireland's preservation is largely attributable to that nation's
"essentially domestic organization," itself an expression of the
Irish faith in the family, the hearthside, and the rural life (76).
The wreckage that marks England's Irish policy is an appropriate

requital for England's incessant efforts to destroy this triad of values. She has worked unremittingly to dissolve and scatter the Irish family; she has destroyed the Irish farmsteads and ruined the land with insane farming techniques; and her international ambitions have tempted her to assimilate Ireland into a make-believe "Empire." England, not the Irish people, is culpable for the present impasse, even in a time of war when the very existence of England is in question: "I entirely sympathize with their being in revolt against the British government. I am in revolt in most ways against the British government myself" (76).

*Irish Impressions* defines the central problem of the post-war world as "What is going to happen to the peasantries?" (35-36). Ireland demonstrates that the peasant system is still viable and that she is insecure only where a capitalist program of landlordship and land rental is allowed to gain a foothold. More serious problems arise with incursions into a peasant economy of big industry, such as may be observed in Belfast, that pustulous sore on the face of beautiful Eire. That Belfast is the seat of Protestantism in Ireland is not lost on Chesterton, but the fact is incidental to his main argument that the ugliness of the city and the arrogance of its citizens are more truly symptomatic of Prussian influence than are Irish-Catholic neutrality and pro-Germanism. The blight of Prussianism evidenced by Belfast is a more serious betrayal of what is English and human, and it can be halted in Ireland and the world only if the peasantry is reinvigorated. The peasant—defined as "the root of the priest, the poet, the warrior"[29]—will bring to modern man the spiritual relief present only in the greatest religion, art, and government.

## V  *The Family and the Home*

Ireland has "turned the corner" because it is the only Western nation that still recognizes the family as the base of the nation. Since the family is the heart of the Irishman's life, he is always defined in terms of his family: he is "the youngest of the Campbells" or "one of the O'Briens." The institution of the family, anchored firmly in the timeless impulses of human nature, is another ideal that requires constant safekeeping from the cor-

rosive effects of modern rationalism. It is the most important
ideal, because other Distributist concepts—those of rural economy, of peasant organization, of private property—are meaningless without a domestic nucleus. The one thing needful is to
invest the family with a power it once had but lost. *Cobbett*
insists that capitalism began the derangement of the family and
of "respectable marriage" by preventing the common man from
saving money (47). Socialism hastened the process of dis-
solution by offering the idea of a state as a rival object of
loyalty.[30] Both systems, by demanding a collectivity of citizens,
have dissipated the internal powers of the family and diminished
its boundaries.

In a number of essays collected in *What's Wrong With the
World* (1910) and in *Fancies versus Fads* (1923), Chesterton
proclaims that the cause of Distributism is inseparable from the
ideal of the family:

The sort of society of which marriage has always been the strongest
pillar is what is sometimes called the distributive society; the society
in which most of the citizens have a tolerable share of property,
especially property in hand. Everywhere, all over the world, the
farm goes with the family and the family with the farm. Unless
the whole domestic group hold together with a sort of loyalty or
local patriotism, unless the inheritance of property is logical and
legitimate, unless the family quarrels are kept out of the courts
of officialism, the tradition of family ownership cannot be handed
on unimpaired.[31]

The operative words are "local patriotism," for Chesterton actual-
ly visualized the family as a small political unit whose purpose
was to protect the individual from the powers of larger political
organizations, including the impersonal State. The family is,
therefore, a buffer between the individual and the anonymous
forces of society.

In *Sidelights*, Chesterton further develops this idea of the
family as a political buffer; in marriage, he says, a man and a
woman form the "only voluntary state" on earth; and, as long
as they are loyal to each other, "they can survive all the vast
changes, deadlocks, and disappointments which make up mere
political history" (81). In *The Thing*, the parents are called

"independent princes" and the children, "subjects"; elsewhere, the father is compared to a "small god" who rules over his "church" or "republic."[32]

Chesterton is sufficiently pragmatic to recognize that, like any political unit within the State, the family derives whatever political power it has from an economic base. This base, in the Distributist system, is provided by the private ownership of farms. Man always thinks, says Chesterton, by an association of ideas, one such cluster being "the elementary things, the land, the roof, the family."[33] This clustering of ideas can be a source of practical political strength since one may appeal to the present Tory party—traditional defenders of the home and family —to willingly partition large property holdings for the sake of the family and the nation.

Sustained by the economic vigor of his farm, the individual can make of his home and family a sanctuary against the state and against the mass organizations beyond the walls of his house. He may spend his time *"refusing* to make a chair or mend a cloak" if he wishes; he is able to set his own course, to "alter arrangements suddenly, make an experiment or indulge in a whim."[34] Chesterton's home is, therefore, a shrine of individuality, anarchy, unreason, and healthful nonsense. The individual in the Distributist system is deified because he rediscovers the spark of divinity that is within him and can act on it: "The average man cannot cut clay into the shape of man; but he can cut earth into the shape of a garden.... Property is merely the art of democracy. It means that every man should have something that he can shape in his own image, as he is shaped in the image of Heaven."[35]

## VI  *Obstacles to Utopia*

To Chesterton, the Distributist ideal has been frustrated because the family as a social and political unit has been undermined by several competing ideals throughout the industrial period. One adversary is the feminist program of the twentieth century, a coda to a large historical tendency to equalize the positions of men and women. Chesterton sardonically observed that the movement had succeeded in making the modern woman a wage-slave equal to her husband. Feminism is always a minor motif in his essays, however, because Chesterton always assumed that only a deluded minority of modern women were listening to the hypnotic Siren-song of equality. Sane women, he hoped, would know their places; they would—in an eighteenth-century mode of speaking that he uses in *What's Wrong With the World*— respect "especially that sanctity and separation of each item which is represented in manners by the idea of dignity and in morals by the idea of chastity" (142).

More ominous is the growing prevalence of divorce, a fact which exasperated Chesterton as much for its social effects as for its religious antinomy. In a pamphlet of 1916, "Divorce versus Democracy," his main complaint was against the injustice of a legal system which permitted the rich to divorce but effectively closed such an alternative to the poor. The real subject of the pamphlet is power, the unequal dispensation of legal rights within society, and, a related subject, the new power granted to a wife in any quarrel with her spouse.

Within a few years, when he devoted a whole book to divorce, *The Superstition of Divorce* (1920—but consisting partly of essays printed in 1918), he was so provoked by the social situation that he detected a capitalist conspiracy behind the spreading prerogative of divorce. His argument is colored with Ruskin's diagnosis of modern fragmentation: "Capitalism, of course, is at war with the family, for the same reason which has led to its being at war with the Trade Unions. This indeed is the only sense in which it is true that capitalism is connected with individualism. Capitalism believes in collectivism for itself and individualism for its enemies. It desires its victims to be individuals, or (in other words) to be atoms."[36]

The plutocracy, Chesterton asserts, encourages divorce because it contributes to the atomization of society which renders the individual worker absolutely vulnerable in a jungle-like labor market. Plutocracy finds its allies in the spurious English dogma of individualism (which Arnold mockingly called "doing as one likes") and feminism, which virtually doubles the number of competing employees in the labor pool. Chesterton's argument is not entirely convincing since one might argue that divorce is *not* in the plutocrat's best interest, that he profits less from a system of easy divorce, resulting in large numbers of unmarried and sporadically vagrant workers, than from a system of rigid marriages, the sources of large families and a steady supply of employees over a number of generations.

The central thesis of *The Superstition of Divorce* is that monstrous economic organizations are using the power of the state to dismantle the traditional powers incorporated in local subcultures, and the main purpose of this scheme is to tamper with the life of the individual. The assault on the holy vow of matrimony leads to the enfeeblement of the family and to the decay of other timeless values of Western culture—filial loyalty, love, mutual respect. As they walk toward their different factories in the morning, husband, wife, and child discharge their love and loyalty to new masters. Chesterton concludes that capitalism is more dangerous than Socialism, in that Socialism "attacks the family" only in theory but capitalism destroys it in practice (75-76).

Although Chesterton is sincere in saying that his book is not based "on the religious argument," his logic leads to the conclusion that the family and the individual can survive only with the help of Christianity, which confirms the existence in each individual of a "strong internal sanctity" (76-77). The only real counterforce to the totalitarian state and to the monopolistic marketplace is "choice, a creative power in the will as well as in the mind." The individual is responsible, finally, for rejecting divorce as an honorable solution to his problems; he must *choose* to restrain himself in the protective confines of the family. By adding his power to that of his loved ones, he loses his vaunted individuality; but he cannot be crushed by the powers of the state.

Without the familial cohesion between individuals, the power of the state will continue its unchecked expansion into the vacuum generated by individualism. The members of society may win the freedom for which they hunger but only to drift helplessly along the stream of a fragmented society. The prevalence of divorce in modern capitalist society is thus an accurate yardstick of the moral resolve in the modern psyche and a portent of the economic and social disaster to come.

## VII   Eugenics and Other Evils

One final menace to the institution of the family was the Eugenics movement, a quasi-scientific program which advocated selective mating and birth control for the purpose of ensuring the transmission of the best qualities of the human race, whatever they may be. Although the Eugenics movement had significant popular and intellectual backing in the early decades of the twentieth century, Chesterton never relaxed his vehement opposition to it; but his most sustained attack appears in *Eugenics and Other Evils* (1922), in which he characterizes Eugenics as another example of the misuse of power. Eugenics he defines as a proposal "to control some families at least as if they were families of slaves."[37] The state will be required, under the hegemony of the Eugenists, to "extend its powers in this area" of the family. The program is the epitome of insanity because, first, Eugenics is admittedly founded on "broken knowledge and bottomless ignorance of heredity" (69) and, second, no one has yet said "who is to control whom." If the Eugenists are equipped with only a half-knowledge, who can give them the authority to execute their program? *Quia custodias custodit*? What are the "best qualities of the human race"? What are the ends men are to aim for if they wish to improve the race?

Eugenics has so far been unchallenged because it is a typical product of an age which has science as a creed and materialism as "our established Church" (77). Neither the scientist nor the materialist is capable of discussing "ends," so he merely waves them aside; the Eugenists' only concern is to put the plan of the moment into action, to exert their power over the individual. Behind it all is conspiracy, of course: the capitalist encourages the Eugenist in the hopes of obtaining the ideal industrial worker—docile, muscular, submissive. "At root," says Chesterton, "the Eugenist is the Employer." Therefore, the Eugenist completes a process inspired by individualism, abetted by feminism, and desired by capitalism: the state intrudes into the private home to measure the health of man and woman and thereby to decide about their right to have children as the result of their love.

*Eugenics and Other Evils* is an astringent book for those

who think of Chesterton as a smiling optimist. The book ends with a cheerless vision of interminable "social and scientific experiment." Eugenics is not a joke, but a serious threat; England has always had a fondness for imbecility, especially when served up with the approval of science. The most challenging threat to Distributism is this Pandora's box placed on England's doorstep by the quack doctors and by the politicians who now have the power to strip the common man of the last vestiges of his liberty.

### VIII   *Assessment*

At this time, one may safely state that Chesterton's Distributist scheme has not come to fruition. Were he alive, he might be able to derive some satisfaction from the apparent demise of Eugenics; once very popular, it has had to retreat in the face of repeated criticism from modern psychology and sociology. Otherwise, the picture for Chesterton would be one of unrelieved darkness. The emigration statistics of Ireland continue to be among the highest in Europe; Hitler's "Thousand Year Reich" (assuming it was an example of Distributism, at least in part) now seems a dim nightmare; industrialization and urbanization have, if anything, accelerated since World War II. The Catholic Church remains the only strong antagonist of divorce, which is in many countries a way of life. It is also fair to conclude that other factors beside divorce—mass communications, an atmosphere of "total war," the paternalism of large business organizations, the mixed benefits accruing from universal education—have contributed to the decline of family life.

Nor has Distributism been without valid criticism, especially because of its psychological and social premises. H. G. Wells argued from the start that Distributism would fail simply because farming success was contingent upon the unpredictable; a farmer with good luck would inevitably gain control of his neighbor's possessions. Julius West traces Distributism back to Samuel Smiles's doctrine of "Self-Help" that now seems to be the very quiddity of Victorian culture; like Smiles, Chesterton haughtily trusts that John Bull can make his living on the countryside, if one just cajoles him long enough.[38] This cavalier disdain for practical considerations is observable in *Culture and the Coming Peril* (1927) in which Chesterton reduces his system to a belief in "the spirit of independence, of thrift, of belief that the individual should earn his own living and stand on his own feet, that he should not be swept away into systems which I call systems of servility" (19).

Chesterton's most unyielding critic, of course, was Bernard Shaw. In the debate published as "Do We Agree?" (1928), Chesterton differentiated Distributism and Socialism in the following manner: "Mr. Bernard Shaw proposes to distribute wealth. We propose to distribute the power." Chesterton compromises his position by admitting that certain powers (mining coal, handling the mail, internal security) must remain with some central authority. Shaw, who quickly sees that the camel has his nose in the tent, challenges his friendly opponent to draw the line where the powers of the state should cease.

Shaw's second argument is even more effective. In any system devised by man, certain inequities are inevitable: if one parcels out two pieces of farmland of equal size, one will be inferior to the other in some way—in moisture, fertility, the amount of sunlight falling on it, convenience of location—and an advantage will settle on one of the farmers. More important, Shaw is aware as Chesterton is not, of the central fact of European culture since 1700: the population explosion. Shaw · realizes that even with the cooperation of the populace, and even if the parcels of land were of equal value, one cannot continue to divide the land indefinitely. One may distribute a patch of land to a peasant, and he may be able to divide it among his sons, but can they then divide it among their children? A plot of land has a lower limit on size beneath which it is not economically self-sustaining. The Distributist aim of "three acres and a cow" cannot be a meaningful ideal during a population explosion.

In spite of these arguments, one need not assume that Distributism was only a beery fancy of the habitués of the pubs along Fleet Street. More than one critic has praised Distributism as a "noble" economic program which starts with an exalted image of man and thus acts as a much-needed corrective for the cynical economic theories of the past century. Chesterton's recommendations for a rehumanization of society, a return to the sense of family and community, and the rediscovery of the worker's individual humanity are vibrant expressions of the human impulses in which they are rooted.

Regrettably for the Distributist theorist, other human impulses enter into the calculations of the human spirit: the need to conform, the urge for security, and the fear of the unknown. A faint shadow of Chesterton's ideal is perhaps cast by the endless migration of urban dwellers to suburban bungalows, but the small ranch house and the fenced yard are only a dim approximation of the Distributist program. In any case, the modern suburbanite seems conspicuously unwilling to exchange the security provided by his large-organization employer for the uncertainties of small farming. With the passage of years, the Distributist ideal recedes farther into dim history; but the concept leaves behind, as a kind of melancholy reminder, the high estimate of man that informed all of Chesterton's writings.

# CHAPTER 4

# *A Sage Too Small for Life*

THE eclipse of Chesterton in this present era is partially attributable to his frequently trumpeted slogan, "All roads lead to Rome." In a latitudinarian age, the slogan smacks too much of militant popery, and its author seems completely enveloped in the armor of Church dogma. Yet Chesterton is not the dogmatist that such a statement appears to intimate. Indeed, while he deplored modern rationalistic thought, which "sprouts and sprawls in every direction," he nevertheless believed that modern man would not accept any philosophy thrust on him from some external authority.[1] Because there is nothing more important in a man's life than his philosophy, the one thing needful in the modern world is a revival of philosophy—that is, a conscientious search by all men for the truth of things.

As for himself, Chesterton boasted that he could "pick up any topic at random, from pork to pyrotechnics, and show that it illustrates the truth of the only true philosophy; so realistic is the remark that all roads lead to Rome."[2] A discussion of Chesterton's total world-view involves not only a treatment of the "Rome" at which he arrived, but a description of the road he followed to get there, as well as some of the pork and pyrotechnics he observed on the way.

One must recognize at the start the impossibility of compressing within a small scope the bewildering intricacy of Chesterton's thought, with all its ramifications and implications. The territory covered by his philosophy deserves lengthy treatment, and, even without the restrictions of space, its totality would elude the grasp of the most careful analysis. Furthermore, Chesterton creates particular problems for the critic because, although a man of reason, he was vigorously paradoxical and also emotional to the point of mysticism. With these cautionary perspectives always in mind, one may attempt a survey of the broad

80

outlines of his philosophical position. As has been noted, Chesterton's relation to modern thought is roughly analogous to that of a Medieval (or early Renaissance) churchman's stand against the rising tide of skepticism and naturalism. Rather than call his world view "Catholic," one might better describe it as "Christian humanism," that central tradition of Western thought since at least 1200 A.D. which combines the often conflicting elements of classical thought and culture and the accepted truths of Christian revelation.

The Christian strain needs little review: it is the commitment to the revelation of the Bible and, in Chesterton's case, the orthodoxy founded on this revelation. The orthodoxy hinges on belief in Adam's Fall, in the resulting state of Original Sin, in man's need for Redemption, in the miracles of the Incarnation and the Virgin Birth, and in Christ's death on the cross for man's sins. All of these beliefs have validity only insofar as they are interpreted by the wisdom of the Catholic Church's central authority.

As numerous scholars have shown, from the thirteenth to seventeenth centuries, Christian artists, theologians, and philosophers attempted to harmonize this Christian faith with various elements of the Classical culture of Greece and Rome. Notably, this meant a revival of interest in Plato and Aristotle (especially for their metaphysics and ethics) and of the Romans Cicero and Seneca (primarily for their ethics). For the artists and the literary men, on the other hand, "humanism" meant the rediscovery of what they believed were the esthetic criteria of the Classical period: balance, clarity of outline and form, proportion, simplicity, dignity of style, and the control of emotions.

Perhaps the most important form of Christian humanism—certainly for Chesterton—was that synthesis achieved by St. Thomas Aquinas in the late thirteenth century. This Thomistic synthesis, which might be called "Christian Aristotelianism," is less "classical" than later Renaissance humanisms, but so was Chesterton's. What St. Thomas attempted to do for the West was to blend into Christianity certain elements of Aristotle's philosophy, of which the following points are crucial: (1) the primacy of being, (2) a vindication of the senses as a source of human knowledge, and (3) the power of man's reason, or philosophy, to reach the truth.[3]

Aquinas's first achievement was to reassert the goodness of this world and this life in opposition to the thought of the Medieval Platonists (who tended to view this world as a poor shadow of some transcendental realm) and the Manicheans (who went further in condemning this world as absolutely worthless and sinful). Aquinas articulated again the traditional Western view that this world is good because it was created by God and partakes of His Goodness, that He intended it to be used by man for good ends and for his pleasure. The second point follows: man is endowed by God with his senses to enjoy the world and to know and extract from it truths for his own benefit. The senses are the primary machinery by which he arrives at these truths; but they are inferior to the reason and should always be under its control. Third, reason is the only guide man has, aside from Faith, to the truth. Man can with his reason prove a number of even the most difficult truths (such as the immortality of the soul and the existence of a providential God) on the basis of his experience in this world.

This Aristotelianism immediately presents difficulties for the Christian theologian and for the practicing Christian. For example, the Augustinian element in Christianity (of which St. Thomas was not entirely free) had traditionally emphasized that the senses were a lower power of man, that had to be controlled very strictly. Particularly troublesome was the Thomistic solution to the problem of reason: man's reason is an instrument of truth, and yet traditionally the reason was considered a feeble light that had been flawed by the Fall of Adam. In Chesterton's case, this view of an undependable reason was available in the works of the great English Christian humanists—Dryden, Pope, Swift, and Dr. Johnson, all of whom he admired. The *locus classicus* of this idea is Swift's assertion (in a letter) that man is not *"Animal rationale"* but, more accurately, *"only rationis capax"*— capable of reason, if he so wishes.[4] Like many Thomists, then, Chesterton is torn between two views: on the one hand, he is anxious to proclaim the holiness of man and his senses, and the strength of his reason; on the other he is aware of the traditional view that reason is often fallacious and incomplete, and must in any case be completed by faith. The result is a central tension between reason and faith, order and emotion, individual experience and outer authority, man and God, that may be observed even in the slightest details of Chesterton's work.

The tension is also visible in the division between Chesterton's "philosophy" and his faith. This is the real significance of his statement, "All roads lead to Rome": the roads are meant to represent the numerous paths by which an individual may arrive at truth with the guidance of the reason, and Rome is the faith which completes and verifies the truths of reason. Although a perfect distinction between reason and faith is impossible (in the Christian view, reason and faith are complementary, not contradictory), such a distinction is convenient for the purposes of orderly discussion. The ambiguity of the relationship between the two explains why Chesterton begins his book *Orthodoxy* (1908) with an analysis of the exact powers of the reason.

## I   Orthodoxy

The fullest presentation of Chesterton's philosophy appears in *Orthodoxy*, said by one critic to be his "most famous, most pregnant and most original book." This work may also be construed as the foundation for all that Chesterton wrote later.[5] He relates that it was written partly to answer those critics (including his brother Cecil) who, having read *Heretics*, dared its author to describe the "orthodoxy" from which those pariahs had strayed.[6] The orthodoxy that emerges is disappointing as theology and surprising for those who may be expecting a strict Romanism. Generously latitudinarian, it admits into the fold anyone willing to subscribe to the Apostles Creed (8). Of course, Chesterton was not pretending to be a professional theologian while writing *Orthodoxy*, a book which might better be interpreted as a spiritual autobiography, the record of one soul's search for truth in the tangle of modern life. Indeed, the book is unsatisfactory as a complete outline of Chesterton's thought. *Orthodoxy* requires the constant reinforcement of evidence available in other books, particularly in four books written within a few years of each other, when Chesterton seems to have been again thinking through his philosophical position. These books are: *Generally Speaking* (1928); *Come to Think of It* (1930); *All Is Grist* (1931); and *The Well and the Shallows* (1935).

The main argument of *Orthodoxy* begins where *Heretics* left off, for it establishes a basic Thomist position against the reason —the human intellect in modern times has been released from all restrictions (faith, authority); it is now endowed with unlimited freedom and power; it is now "free to destroy itself" (43). The brake once provided by religious faith and by the eternal verities is now gone, and the force of reason drives onward, questioning everything until it questions itself. The dead end has been reached: the rancid skepticism that poisons the modern world. One idea erases another, one fashionable school replaces another for a brief moment, and reason seems everywhere impotent because it does not know where to stop. Man finds himself lost because there is no other authority to balance and curb the power of the reason.

Chesterton finds this excessive rationalism perplexing because there is no justification—either in Western theology or in modern science—for its exalted state. From the dominant scientific viewpoint of the nineteenth century, reason differs only in degree from the faculties of a chimpanzee; it is a feeble light evolved from the slime of prehistoric swamps. From a theological position, as has been seen, man's reason has been compromised since the Fall of Adam, and it has always needed the corrective influence of revelation. Modern man is notoriously unable to think through the implications of his vaunted scientific knowledge, and he has lost his belief in Adam's Fall. On two counts, then, he has lost his healthy skepticism about the power of reason; and he is now sinking under a welter of theory, argument, debate, and intellectual chaos. Chesterton repeats, "I said that our mental ruin has been wrought by wild reason, not by wild imagination" (52).

Another modern heresy that needs reproof—a heresy that lies in exactly the opposite direction—is the "romantic" tradition inherited from the nineteenth century, one which tends to denigrate the power of the reason; in some cases, Romanticism denies it entirely, stressing instead the emotions or the imagination as central guides to truth. Too often this Romanticism has declined into such horrors as the Dionysiac and Prussian philosophies of the twentieth century. Thus Chesterton—like a good Victorian Dissenter—is always ready to assail the sexual element of man, "a fury that we cannot afford to inflame." He found D. H. Lawrence reprehensible for telling his readers "to rebel against reason and rely entirely upon instinct and emotion."[7] Almost beneath contempt was Freud, whose "occult" science has contributed to the "breakdown at once of the idea of reason and of the idea of authority."[8]

Chesterton stands, as has been noted, between the two extremes of those who place too much faith in the reason and those who would deny it entirely.[9] Most dangerous, in Chesterton's view, are those who pervert the reason by not understanding its proper functions and limits. The modern emphasis on empiricism, on facts, and on methodology results in a diminished version of rationalism—indeed, in a philosophy which is irrationalistic and anti-intellectual, as Whitehead has observed. To Chesterton, modern man's passion for facts and for the inductive method is precisely the cause of anarchy of thought and a dehumanized society. Men have lost themselves in a haystack of facts amassed by the Baconian methodology that has been triumphant since the Renaissance.

This mania for induction is, to Chesterton, laughably inferior to the Medieval schoolman's ability to think through complex relations with the data of empirical facts.[10] Today, Chesterton complains, one must listen to numbers of pottering eccentrics anxious to prove that Shakespeare's plays were written by Bacon or by Queen Elizabeth, that a woman wrote Homer's epics, or that the Great Pyramid predicted the Great War. Worse, scientific method is so fashionable that it arrogantly forces its way into areas where it is not wanted, as in the case of the Eugenist who insolently attempts to dictate who shall marry and who shall not on the basis of shattered knowledge. Meanwhile, psychologists, who claim to cure the soul without believing in it, are guided only by a definition of spiritual "goodness" that can be summed up by the mockingly contradictory phrase, "polymorphous perversity."

Chesterton's arguments strike out in the direction of the Romantic philosophy; he is, he says, an "old fashioned person" who believes that reason is a "gift of God and a guide to truth."[11] In the other direction, his argument is against the scientist, the empiricist, the statistician. One can neither deny the reason its

rightful scope of action, as the Romantic tends to do, nor, like
the rationalist, credit it with powers it does not have. Exactly
what the proper balance is, is difficult for Chesterton to say.
True reason is defined (in *The Well and the Shallows*) rather
nebulously as "the ordinary common daylight of intellectual
instinct."[12] Since "all men are equal in the possession of human
reason,"[13] it does not have the accuracy, indeed the infallibility,
of abstract logic; on the other hand, one does not lose oneself
in it, as one may easily do in the emotions or in empirical data.
When a man uses his reason, his full being is called into play—
his emotions, his imagination, his knowledge of past history (as
well as the immediate situation), and the wisdom of the human
race. One of the paradoxes of Christian humanism, then, is that
it continually warns against the irrational elements in man's
nature—his senses, his passions, the erring ways of the reason—
while at the same time recommending other non-rational elements as a check on the reason: faith, the self-abasement before
dogma, and the mysteries of the Church.

For Chesterton, Original Sin may be defined as Pride, especially the pride of reason, the failure of man to recognize his
limits. Pride can be curbed by restraining the reason within
the limits defined by dogma and the authority of the Church.
Such counsel will be rejected by the modern secularist, who
will call it "tyrannical and repressive"; but Chesterton argues in
*Orthodoxy* that dogma and authority fulfill a vital psychological
and epistemological purpose: "The authority of priests to
absolve, the authority of popes to define the authority, even of
inquisitors to terrify; these were all only dark defences erected
round one central authority, more undemonstrable, more supernatural than all—the authority of a man to think" (45).

Chesterton's argument—as the above statement suggests—is
not exclusively religious, although an occasional argument in
*Orthodoxy* may raise religious implications, as when he claims
that the problems of the West began when man attempted "to
pull the mitre off pontifical man; and his head has come off with
it" (46). The originality of *Orthodoxy* rests partly in its emphasis
on "secular" truths or dogmas incarnate as much in the folklore
of the past and in the popular arts of the present as in the
doctrines of organized religion. Chesterton tells the reader that

he can discover the truth about man that is "at least relatively real"[14] in the trivial folktales, legends, and myths that we heard in our childhood. With these truths we can test the fashionable truths of the day and the decisions which we are apt to make on the basis of half-digested fact and the selfish impulse of the moment. The purpose of education should be to preserve this literature (this "teeming vitality of the dead"), which then is the shield that prevents the destruction of any social institution or general concept until the history and purpose of each have been understood.

Tradition—or the perspectives on the truth that men unearth by reading fairy tales, legends, neighborhood stories, and myths— makes up a kind of "inheritance from human history." Supplementing tradition may be the current literature of the common man, such as detective stories, music-hall melodramas, popular jokes, and farces. Among Chesterton's earliest articles for *The Speaker* (collected as *The Defendant,* 1901) were a number of pieces which espoused such trivia, "The Philosophy of Penny Dreadfuls," "The Philosophy of Farce," "Defence of Slang," and "The Value of Detective Stories." These essays were not just the scribblings of a poseur; numerous friends have spoken of Chesterton's collection of penny-dreadfuls and his lifelong habit of reading whatever "trash" was at hand. He was never so serious as when he announced in *Orthodoxy* that "We all owe much sound morality to the penny dreadfuls" (105).

## II  *Ends and Means*

The fundamental intellectual task for Chesterton was nothing less than the redemption of the world. The recorded literature of the Romantic and Victorian periods shows that for Western man the industrial world had been despiritualized, emptied of all meaning and worth by the inexorable march of science. Man's mounting accumulation of empirical knowledge had led him into a coma of ennui. Following the advice of Bacon, modern man had taken all knowledge as his province; but the accretion of billions of facts, an infinity of phenomena, had drained each particle of life of whatever value it traditionally had held. In a coral reef, which polyp is most distinguished

or important? In the modern nightmare of living, men sleepwalk
with their senses turned off, are uncertain of their own worth,
and are insensible to the miracles of life surrounding them. In
an interview, Chesterton said that the "primary problem for
me was the problem of how men could be made to realize the
wonder and splendour of being alive."[15] One is tempted to say
that this was the very problem faced by St. Thomas in the thirteenth century.

In *Orthodoxy*, Chesterton, having warned against the exclusive
power of man's rationalism, assumes "this desirability of an
active and imaginative life, picturesque and full of a poetical
curiosity, a life such as western man at any rate always seems
to have desired" (4). The two-fold task, then, is to restrain the
power of the intellect—now running free wildly, like a flywheel
without a governor—and to renew a sacramental view of the
universe in which each phenomenon is discerned as "miraculous"
and therefore as divine. Both aims can be achieved by a single
act: the rediscovery of "proper first principles," the absence of
which explains the insanity of the twentieth century. In literary
criticism, for example, because critics have no ideal of the
Beautiful, true criticism is impossible; and the critic lapses into
puffery or impressionism. Similarly, modern plutocracy hails the
virtues of "service" and "efficiency," but it wisely conceals the
ends for which men must be efficient: "It all comes back to
whether we do propose to worship the end; and preferably the
right end."[16]

The reader may at this point justifiably ask where men are
to obtain the knowledge of such "ends." For Chesterton the
humanist, the principles are readily available in the eternal
standards of truth—moral, esthetic, philosophical—found in the
Catholic Church, in the traditions of men, in folklore, and in
man's full use of his reason. Anathema is Hamlet's relativistic
witticism, "There's nothing either good or bad but thinking
makes it so." On the contrary, Chesterton unabashedly uses
the words "true" and "truth" in his works, thereby haughtily
dividing various sheep from goats, the truth-tellers from the
deceivers. He proclaims that the ideas of Medieval Christians
are "still true," while the ideas of modern Protestants can be
rejected because they are "simply, completely untrue." On

nothing is he more adamant than that "it is not true that the idea of right and wrong changes."[17]

A disputant may ask how one may account for the displacement of these "eternal" truths by more "modern" (and fallacious) ideas. Chesterton's answer is that modern man lives in a "chaotic and ill-educated time," and that he urgently needs to reestablish an educational system which "should give a man abstract and eternal standards by which he can judge material and fugitive conditions."[18] Furthermore, there is a kind of conspiracy by historians who have obscured the eternal truths— "so obvious and enormous"—with half-truths and outright lies.[19]

The sharp distinction between the timeless and the transitory, and the prescription of education as a discipline of the mind, led Chesterton again to a defense of tradition and the test of time as a measure of truth. A central passage in *Orthodoxy* affirms the sanity of tradition (note that the argument is secular), which "refuses to submit to the small and arrogant oligarchy of those who merely happen to be walking about" (70). Education cradles and protects tradition, "handing it on with a voice of authority." "That is the one eternal education: to be sure enough that something is true that you dare to tell it to a child."[20] (The argument is open to serious objection, however, for how can one be "sure enough"? Is it a matter of *feeling* sure? Might not an authoritative, dogmatic style of education be a dissimulation of inner uncertainty or error?)

### III   *First Principle: Limitation*

As for the important ends, the eternal Truths which may be discovered in tradition, custom, and the experience of mankind, Chesterton's answer creates a philosophical stance, which, if not entirely systematic or original, demands close attention because of its presence throughout his speculative and fictional works. Having discussed in *Orthodoxy* the divinity of the reason and its paradoxical unreliability, Chesterton announces one of the central principles of his philosophy: "The moment you step into the world of facts, you step into a world of limits" (57). Chesterton's is a secularized version of the doctrine of the Fall, declaring as it does that "there are certain laws and limits to the mind." Again, such a view rebuts the two mainstreams of modern thought: science, which glorifies the "march of mind" to some inevitable Utopia, and Romanticism, which praises the autonomy of "man's unconquerable mind."

The inherent limitation of the mind may be described as acting to reduce its effectiveness whenever it is forced to deal with subjects too large for it; a native impulse toward self-control, identified by wise men in all ages, is reinforced by the external aids—organizations, dogmas, laws, codes, censorship—which man has sensibly provided for himself to permit the mind freedom to work in a circumscribed area. Chesterton believes that where man has broken free of such limitations, internal or external, he has destroyed himself. The inductive method of science has created an intellectual chaos by making man confront an infinity of phenomena in the universe. Conversely, the various theories of the imagination disseminated by the Romantic movement have encouraged men to lose themselves in the empyrean and have brought him to the edge of madness by having him lose all touch with reality and a sense of order.

At this point, Chesterton leaves the Romantic theorists in the airless expanses of pure spirit and infinite space, and he counterpoises the Thomistic view that "the true spiral of imagination and creation is always twisting inwards towards smaller and smaller things, ever since men realized that jewels were smaller than pebbles and seeds smaller than clods; that if there be indeed a progress of humanity it may be such a progress to discover its own heart."[21] One is reminded on the one hand of Blake's admonition "To see the Universe in a grain of Sand" and on the other of Eliot's definition of Classicism as "To concentrate and not to dissipate."

Chesterton's theory of the imagination is deliberately naïve and even provincial, for it prefers the freedom within limits of the child to the boundless expansionism of the Romantic spirit. This self-limiting attitude is the secret of Chesterton's identification with the child and the delights of childhood, the toy theater, the literature of make-believe: "It is plain on the face of the facts that the child is positively in love with limits. He uses his imagination to invent imaginary limits." This childish imagination may be likened to a lens that brings the rays of the

sun together into a bright and burning spot of intense vision.
"If anybody chooses to say that I have founded all my social
philosophy on the antics of a baby, I am quite satisfied to bow
and smile."[22]

One has already observed Chesterton's application of this
almost-Classical principle of limitation to contemporary social
and political problems. He denounced bigness in all its forms—
in populations, nations, businesses, and organizations. One is
reminded that his first appearance in public was as a combatant
against Imperialism in the controversy over the Boer War. He
remained skeptical all his life of England's quest for Empire,
of plans for "Federations of Nations," of such modern theorizing
as Tolstoy's "love of general humanity."[23] One recalls Swift's
*confessio* also, that "principally I hate and detest that animal
called man, although I heartily love John, Peter, Thomas, and
so forth."

Chesterton's political imagination constantly spiralled inwards,
from Great Britain, to England and Scotland, to Ireland and
Wales, to local counties, and then to the histories and cultures
of villages.[24] One historian relates that Chesterton would often
buy a railroad ticket to some small village whose name intrigued
him and then journey there (often without informing his wife)
in search of adventure; in effect, he was disappearing into a
mysterious reality in order to know it.[25]

Thus the principle of smallness, the belief that a thing needed
to be small in order to be known and loved, was carried into all
corners of Chesterton's thought. The small thing enabled the
mind to grasp, to concentrate, to know, because the small thing
is clear, direct, and specific. "The Universe itself cannot show us
its unity; we have to judge it in selections."[26] Infinity is an evil,
no matter how impressive or imposing.


## IV   *Second Principle: Discreteness*

Chesterton's second great truth, discreteness, is implied somewhat in the first, limitation. In art, literature, economy, politics,
and religion, Chesterton disliked vagueness of outline and diffuse-
ness; he demands that the objects of vision be clearly outlined
against a background. One may interpret this principle as a re-

statement of Classical esthetics or as a reflection of the Thomistic trust in the senses. Chesterton's defense of private property is also implicit in this epistemological principle on the theory that private property may be defined as a circle drawn around *meum* (what is mine), separating it from *tuum* (what is yours).[27] The small village has more beauty and integrity than a large, undefined mass like London (Cobbett's "Great Wen").[28]

Whatever is formless and shapeless is not simply odious but un-Western, dangerous. The achievements of the French Impressionists Chesterton considered paltry because they all contributed to breaking down form with light; and he was similarly wary of the cinema, which is impressionism applied to movement, the shattering of solid forms on celluloid.[29] His argument with evolution is based as much on this principle as on any religious considerations: evolution invokes a breakdown of barriers, and the species are no longer solid categories but evanescent classes that blend into each other.[30]

The principle, however, is equally applicable to matters of religion. In a number of essays Chesterton vents his wrath against those religions which ignore the principle of discreteness somewhere in their doctrines: Pantheism, which merges spirit and body, God and nature, man and animal; Eastern Transcendentalism, which teaches the individual ways of becoming "absorbed into the unity of all things" ("a loathsome fancy," adds Chesterton); Islam, which reduces man to nothing by erasing his individuality in the blinding light and power of One God.[31]

## V  *Third Principle: Complexity*

The first two eternal verities, the principles of limitation and discreteness, are apparently contradicted or at least seriously qualified by a third principle: that of complexity. Chesterton is especially determined to combat the modern rationalistic tendency to oversimplify—to create simplistic abstractions or single-minded approaches to life which ignore the variety and multifariousness of God's Creation.[32] Western man historically has been uniquely capable of recognizing this complexity in life, but he now seems to be losing the gift under the impact of his pragmatic civilization. Chesterton deplores the simplistic thinking, for example, of the Moslem mind, which ignores the profound implications of the Incarnation and the Trinity by reducing religion to the worship of One God, all of life to spirit, and all of man's experiences to the fact of fatalism.[33] What is ominous is that European culture presently seems to have fallen under the spell of similar abstractions or paradigms.

"There is a real sense," says Chesterton, "in which modern things tend to simplicity."[34] His quarrel with the "heretics" arose from his belief that the theories they hawked in the marketplace—evolution, progress, materialism, pragmatism, estheticism, even racism—were simplistic, only feeble embodiments of part of the whole Truth. They were all one-sided concepts that only imperfectly sketched out one side of the complex multiformity of the universe.

Chesterton's advice seems to be, "Let a thousand flowers bloom." He seems to argue for a philosophy of pluralism, and he certainly recommends a kind of unconscious acceptance (without the need of understanding or of imposing a final order) of the diversity of life. Yet this liberal view is contradicted by a simplistic current of another type that is everywhere evident in Chesterton's work. It has been noted, for example, that his theory of language is reductionist, requiring that a word mean only one thing. He prefers art which, like the paintings of Watts, focuses on a single, clearly discernible form, rather than the shimmering disjunctions of Impressionistic or Cubist works. He admires democracy, but only on a small scale, and preferably without those pluralistic elements (such as the Jews) that sully the Arcadian homogeneity.

Chesterton's philosophy is therefore not a consistently pluralistic one; certain limits or controls must constantly be imposed on the deluge of experience which threatens to overwhelm the individual. The problem is one of limits: how much variety or complexity can the individual mind absorb and control before it is crushed under the burden? How much complexity is permitted, and where does one draw the line?

## VI  *Fourth Principle: Proportion*

While recognizing the polymorphism of the universe and the boundless arena of action provided for man, Chesterton's philosophy takes equal cognizance of the limitations of the human mind. A certain balance or proportion of elements must occur in man's experience, in the body politic, and in the ethics which man uses to shape his life. Chesterton's recognition of proportion reflects both the Aristotelian component in his Thomism and the humanistic stress on Classical balance. Whatever its sources, Chesterton is thoroughly committed to its defense; he calls proportion a "thing as invisible as beauty, as inscrutable as God."[35] The individual must exert himself to establish his own inward balance by recognizing the often discordant impulses of optimism and pessimism, pride and humility, body and spirit. This personal struggle of the individual must be facilitated by the educational system, whose primary function is to instill in man a sense of balance and a love of a variety of things in life.[36]

To Chesterton, the heresies of all times, the heresies of the modern age, result from the failure of their proponents to maintain a balance in themselves and their thought. Mohammed teaches the Omnipotence of God, but forgets the glory of man; Calvin stresses God's foreknowledge and the predestination of man, but ignores free will; Hinduism treats man as though he were all soul and no flesh. The triumph of materialism in the twentieth century is a "sort of insane simplicity,"[37] and it takes no great genius to detect the serious imbalance of such philosophies as Decadent sensualism or the determinism of Marx.

The problem of integrating matter and spirit—of finding the proper proportion of each in man's life—is a particularly vexing one for Chesterton, just as it was for St. Thomas, Plato, Aristotle, and practically every other philosopher. In Chesterton's work, including *Orthodoxy*, the problem may be stated thus: if one is to regain a sacramental view of the world, how does one explain, how can one explain, the infusing of matter with spirit? At the least, one is forced to prevent the exclusion of one by the other. Chesterton found that he had a number of allies in the fight against Victorian (and Edwardian) materialism; but unanticipated was his almost solitary stand against an all-encompassing spiritualism. Thus the reader may find it strange that Chesterton occupied himself so much with various heresies of the Ideal or Spiritual—spiritualism in religion, formalism in art, statistics in politics and government, and an increasingly fashionable Orientalism.

To such forms of spiritualism (or "Platonism") in his time, Chesterton boldly opposes Thomism or a proto-existentialism. In *The Resurrection of Rome,* he asserts that "the ideal" is the curse of Hellas on European culture; "for the ideal can be more hardening or even brutalising than the real.... Plato dealt with babies in batches like the statisticians of Birth Control" (70). The modern stock market is a plutocratic evil that is symptomatic of our society: it works insanely with arithmetical figures, charts, and graphs; but it is forgetful of the pigs, pigiron, and hungry men concealed behind those abstractions.[38]

Chesterton claims that all of Western culture—that the Western soul—began with Pope Gregory III's quarrel with the Iconoclasts, that heretical sect which (influenced by Islamic proscriptions against religious art) was bent on cleansing the Catholic Church of its images. As Chesterton tells the story, Pope Gregory successfully defended the Church's traditional acceptance of this world's reality; and he thus sanctioned the ever-recurring marriage of spirit and matter in the art of the West. Figuratively, Gregory "stirred up the mud and started the stream that was to be our own story."[39]

The acceptance of "mud"—of concrete reality, of the objectivity of this world—aligns Chesterton with a number of his literary heroes, Dickens, Browning, Chaucer, all of whom taught in different ways that reality should be accepted with all its ugliness and deformity. More important, Chesterton may be placed squarely in the Thomist tradition since, like Aquinas, he states that all philosophy must begin with concrete sense experience. Both Chesterton and Aquinas affirm that, while the ultimate object of Man is God, the immediate object of the mind is the material thing; the mind cannot churn away endlessly trying to make something of abstractions and ideals. It is theologically and psychologically indispensable for the individual to observe life, love it, know it, and to arrive at some knowledge of God through his observations and his reason. This love of "solid and human and reasonable things" is not mere whimsy on Chesterton's part, but reflects his belief in the mutual interpenetration of spirit and matter. Only in the reality of life, crude and sordid as it is, can the spirit abide.

## VII  *Consequence: Immanence*

At this point in *Orthodoxy*—in the chapter "The Ethics of Elfland"—Chesterton's argument bounds forward to the answer to his philosophical problem, "how men could be made to realize the splendour of being alive." The discussion teeters for a moment on the indistinct boundary between philosophy and religion, but it does not as yet pass over. What he discovered for himself is the "fact" of immanence—that spirit does reside in matter and that man's only logical response to this knowledge is awe and gratitude. This "natural religion" is admittedly not original; it was a "startling discovery" but "the whole thing had been discovered before. It had been discovered by Christianity"(70). The heart of this discovery is that "Ordinary things are more valuable than extraordinary things; nay, they are more extraordinary" (67). The tragedy is that modern man has lost his capacity for wonder in a universe which is marvelous simply because *it is*. The acedia of modern man (the sleep-walking attitude mentioned earlier) is apparently the illogical effect of modern science: the engulfment which the soul feels in a universe of infinite size, and the ennui created by the observation of the repetitive operations of nature (90-98).

Chesterton's main quarrel is directed at man's jaded response to the repetitions of nature. He has ceased to see the "miracles" of nature—leaves falling in autumn, the sun rising each morning, the marvelous repetition of birth—simply because they have been repeated an infinite number of times. Misled by the resemblance of nature to a mechanical process, man has turned the universe into a machine, that watch-universe which Bishop Paley admired so much as evidence of a Supreme Watchmaker, but which Carlyle more despairingly described as a Universe "all void of Life, of Purpose, of Volition, even of Hostility: it was one, huge, dead, immeasurable Steam-engine rolling on, in its dead indifference to grind me limb from limb."[40] By accurately measuring, charting, and analyzing the universe, modern man has transmuted it into an abstract process, and emptied it of spirit and meaning.

Chesterton's attitude is a variety of mysticism: the only stance one can take toward the universe is one of rapt awe, something like Tertullian's *credo quia est impossible*. Far from desiring more knowledge, Chesterton prefers to remain in ignorance: "I am quite comfortable in a completely mysterious cosmos."[41] Knowledge is Pride, and Pride is Original Sin. Thus he also struggles to press that mystery into the most inconsequential corners of the universe, advocating a "necessary mood of astonishment at everything outside one's soul—even one's own body," and even the sight of one's boots.[42] In this delight in the world and in the desire to live life to its fullest, Chesterton paradoxically echoes that Decadent tradition that he deplored so heartily, and especially Walter Pater's invitation to live with a hard, gemlike flame.

To Chesterton, the preacher of *Ecclesiastes* was wrong to react to the processes of Nature with the despairing lament, "*Vanitas vanitatum*." It may be that God loves repetition—millions of daffodils, housecats, leaves of grass, and sunsets. With man's limited capacity, he fails to see that each item among the millions of natural phenomena has divinity stamped in it; this blindness is, however, to be expected of man's fallen state. "There are certain laws and limits to the mind. . . . There is such a thing as concentration; there is such a thing as contrast; there is such a thing as proportion, there is emphatically such a thing as boredom."[43] The holiness of each object explains why Chesterton wrote essays on "Cheese," "A Piece of Chalk," and "What I found in my Pocket."

The argument in *Orthodoxy* shifts from a rational plane to an emotional one, from philosophy to religion, as Chesterton hypothesizes that the regular rising of the sun "might be due not to a lifelessness, but to a rush of life." The magical quality that he has discovered in the universe has been called Immanence (and, incorrectly, Incarnation), the in-dwelling of the spirit. The argument reaches a Whitman-like ecstasy (and Whitman was Chesterton's favorite poet in his youth): "But the repetition in Nature seemed sometimes to be an excited repetition, like that of an angry schoolmaster saying the same thing over and over again. The grass seemed signalling to me with all its fingers at once; the crowded stars seemed bent upon being understood. The sun would make me see him if he rose a thousand times. The recurrences of the universe rose to the maddening rhythm of an incantation."

## VIII   Conclusion

Chesterton's discovery of the holiness of all reality, of the immanence of spirit in matter, has been achieved entirely through the mediation of the reason. At this stage of the argument, Chesterton confesses his delight in having made the discovery and that "it had been discovered by Christianity." As philosophy becomes subsumed under religion, one may conveniently take stock of what has been accomplished.

It is clear that several major preoccupations of Western philosophy converge in Chesterton's *Orthodoxy* and in the essays that support it. The influence of St. Thomas Aquinas has been discussed at some length. In addition to what has been said, however, one may point to the influence of St. Thomas's esthetic theory, in which he defines the elements of beauty as *integritas* —wholeness, integrity, one thing; *consonantia*—harmony, proportion; and *claritas*—clarity, intelligibility. Do these not resemble Chesterton's central epistemological and psychological principles —limitation, discreteness, and proportion?[44]

Chesterton's more recent predecessors (although it is unlikely that he had read their works) were such men as Kierkegaard, who had fought the tyranny of rationalism, and Dostoyevsky, who found hope for salvation in the very unpredictability of man. Like them, Chesterton refused to believe that man might be programmed by computers or nature be reduced to statistics. Always at the bottom of human experience there would be an element of mystery and irrationality to slake our dry spirits.

The weaknesses in Chesterton's argument (however attractive its intentions) do not need detailed explication. Certainly the weakest point is his handling of nature's repetitions as "miraculous"; a miracle is, by definition, a singular event in human life or nature that can only be explained by recourse to a deity. To use it in any other sense is to be irresponsible with words. To say that the sun's rising is a miracle is a fallacious argument because the event is given a connotation (that it was divinely caused), and then a conclusion is built on the connotation: that there is indeed a deity. Furthermore, it does little good to insist that the rising of the sun is "wonderful" and "miraculous" even though the phenomenon has been repeated a million times. It may be true, but the human being who has seen it several times, or a hundred times, will not believe it; and he will not rise early to see it. So true is the old folk-saying, which Chesterton should have heeded, that familiarity breeds contempt.

Worse is to follow. Up to this point Chesterton has had to struggle against the heretics and agnostics; when he is inspired by the atmosphere of combat, he writes wittily, concretely, and forcefully. His knack for finding the right example, the right analogy to make an abstruse point is unique in English letters; it also reminds one of St. Thomas's view that analogy was a fundamental process by which the mind could reach God.

Regrettably, the fascination of the struggle is over as soon as Chesterton recognizes the existence of a God who acts through nature: "The spike of dogma fitted exactly into the hole in the world—it had evidently been meant to go there—and then the strange thing began to happen. When once these two parts of the two machines had come together, one after another, all the other parts fitted and fell in with an eerie exactitude. I could hear bolt after bolt over all the machinery falling into its place with a kind of click of relief. Having got one part right, all the other parts were repeating that rectitude, as clock after clock strikes noon. Instinct after instinct was answered by doctrine after doctrine" (128).

It is a fine image, but the mechanical metaphor bodes ill for what is to come; the narrow path of the individual is suddenly broadened into a wide highway in which the combative Chesterton is lost. All the drama, originality, and personality disappear; the style of the writing degenerates into bombast or treacle (as may be seen in the second half of *Orthodoxy*, for example). For the non-believers and Protestants—and for some Catholics—Chesterton is never so rewarding or amusing in his religious expositions as in the writings which describe his philosophical quest. One Catholic critic has said that Chesterton has done more harm than good to the cause of the Catholic Church, by erasing with his complacency and jocularity all that was painfully carved out by Cardinal Newman.[45]

## CHAPTER 5

# Doctor of the Church

### I Orthodoxy

ABOUT halfway through *Orthodoxy*, Chesterton pauses to reflect that "all this time I had not even thought of Christian theology" (102). His spiritual odyssey had, until this point, been more philosophical than theological; from this point on, we are given an extended discussion of the specifically religious problems that troubled Chesterton and his age. The first half of *Orthodoxy* (and many of his early essays) show Chesterton's struggle with an intellectual problem at least two centuries old: how to reestablish God in His universe, reinvest the world with spirit (and "magic"), and restore some meaning to man's life. Chesterton had carefully established a doctrine of Immanence by which God was seen working in and through Nature. The largeness of the universe and the deadening repetitions of nature's processes were miraculous signs of God's presence and also unarguable vindication of St. Thomas's first and second proofs of the existence of God. Far from being the absentee landlord of the Deists and mechanists, God gives more evidence for hope: "There was something personal in the world, as in a work of art" (101). All the processes of life, however repetitious, "might be due not to lifelessness, but to a rush of life."

The skeptic may argue that such Immanence is mere fantasy or day-dreaming. A more serious objection to Chesterton's argument is that, as a good Christian, he cannot consistently harbor such fantasies, for latent in this Romantic Immanency is the disturbing heresy of Pantheism. Because Chesterton senses that his argument is toppling over into "natural religion" (the worship of natural objects arising from the recognition of the "holiness" of all things in nature), he reverses his direction in the chapter "The Flag of the World," to refute with vehemence the numerous versions of the Pantheistic heresy.

101

Beneath the cataract of words, the skeletal argument is that
nature provides man with no religious or ethical guide because
of its multifariousness; anyone committed to a "natural religion"
can find evidence in nature for acting however he wishes:
"Pantheism is all right as long as it is the worship of Pan. But
Nature has another side which experience and sin are slow in
finding out, and it is no flippancy to say of the god Pan that he
soon showed the cloven hoof. The only objection to Natural
Religion is that somehow it always becomes unnatural" (123).
This familiar Christian concept argues that physical nature is
fallen with Adam, and is different from and inferior to a spiritual
realm. The reader begins to see nature stripped of magic and
goodness, and finds that Chesterton has begun to undermine
all that he had laboriously constructed in the first four chapters.

The Pantheist believes that God is "*in* all things," but Christian
theism, says Chesterton wisely teaches that God is a Creator
who retired from His creation; when He had completed His
works, he "sundered" Himself from the world. All creation (like
procreation) is a "breaking off," performed "like the slash of a
sword" (125). Chesterton feels impelled to emphasize this
divorce of God and creation because only in this way can he
prove that man has free will; with God divorced from his creation, man is free to make his own destiny. In solving the problem of free will, however, Chesterton is forced back to the
original problem: a Deity that is not Immanent but Transcendent, and a physical universe that is again emptied of Spirit:
"That transcendence and distinctness of the deity ... was really
the only reason why any one wanted to be a Christian." The
Deity's "rush" into the machine had proven only temporary, for
He immediately retreated to some distant corner. With this retir-
ing Creator, man is in danger of arriving again at the Islamic
Deity—blindingly transcendent and aloof to man and creation—
or the God of the Deists who permits the universal engine to operate by natural laws. In closing the door on one implication of his
logic, Chesterton permits another—the despiritualized universe
he was originally rebutting—to reappear at another entrance.

Plainly, Chesterton has to restore God to the Universe. He
attempts to do so in the next chapter, "The Paradoxes of Christianity," in which the comforts of revelation are eagerly seized

upon. The solution to the theological dilemma is not Immanence, which proved so dangerous, but Incarnation: "Christ was not a being apart from God and man, like an elf, nor yet a being half human and half not, like a centaur, but both things at once and both things thoroughly, very man and very God" (152). This wholehearted embracing of revelation permits Chesterton to thrust the troublesome problem of Pantheism out of sight. Whether or not the rest of the universe, aside from Christ, is also divine in any real sense remains unanswered.

"The Paradoxes of Christianity" supports Christian revelation with a reasoned proof that Chesterton repeated on a number of occasions. The argument asserts that Christian revelation must be the Truth because its detractors have accused it of diametrically opposed weaknesses, errors, or fallacies. Some have accused it of preaching unmanly weakness, others blame it for causing the most internecine wars in history; some have called it otherworldly, while others have abominated its thirst for worldly power and goods; some dislike the asceticism it preaches, yet others are horrified by its pomp and ceremony. Chesterton concludes that, because these arguments directly contradict each other, the Christian Church must be resting at some center of truth, thereby achieving a kind of reconciliation of opposites which the critics, being humanly imperfect, cannot fully see or comprehend. The Church—a large, rugged rock of dogma, delicately poised—permits the full play of all kinds of passions, impulses, differences of opinion, and personal philosophies (164).

Chesterton's argument has a spurious attractiveness, for who would not wish that truth might be triangulated in such a fashion? The argument is open to serious objection, however, because the same argument might be applied to any major religion, each of which might be described as a rock delicately poised, each permitting a limited amount of individual freedom within a rigid framework. More seriously, the argument distorts the essence of Pauline Christianity, which, like other codes, teaches that some impulses of human nature cannot be tolerated but must be completely eradicated. Certainly Chesterton would have to admit that Christianity hardly tolerates or welcomes the passions of hatred, lust, or gluttony as dynamic opposites to other inhuman impulses. Like all religions, Christianity has its own standards by which it excludes or entirely forbids; to the extent that it excludes, it is incomplete, and its center may therefore appear to be a false center to the unbeliever observing it from the outside.

As for the purpose of man in a world in which the truth of the Incarnation is accepted, Chesterton, always a man of his Western culture, rejects such alternatives as Hinduism and evolution; to him, there is something unholy about Hindu inwardness and its sense of fatalism, and evolution itself leads only to chaos.[1] Man creates history by following the Carlylean doctrine that "This is not a world, but the materials for a world." If the world is God's creation, how much should man alter, and how much dutifully accept? Chesterton's answer is a vague compromise: man must be neither too fast nor too slow, but he must show a "certain amount of restraint and respect, a certain amount of energy and mastery" (191).

So much for the means. What is the end of man's effort? What is the ideal toward which he aims? Man's vision of where the world should go, or what it should be, is directed by what "is called Eden" (184). Chesterton does not elaborate, but this ideal plainly includes a recognition of man's fallen state and his subordination to God's will. With the opening provided by the myth of Eden, Chesterton proceeds in the next pages to expound the full panoply of the Christian world-view—the existence of God, the pride of Lucifer, the rebellion of Hell, the fall of Adam, and the separation of Man and Nature.

The penultimate chapter of *Orthodoxy* provides an answer to the nagging question about the extent to which man can determine his fate and shape his environment. For Chesterton has no doubt that man is endowed with free will to do as he wishes. The dogmas of the Christian Church and the narrative literature unique to the West (unique in the creation of fictional beings who display free will) enshrine this fundamental dogma. Only the heresies of East and West, ancient and modern, deny it: Islam and Kismet, Calvinism and predestination, modern behaviorists, and Freudians (233). The current fashionable jargon about events as "inevitable" or conditions as "incurable" have convinced men that they cannot help themselves; as a result, things get worse. Chesterton affirms repeatedly that all reform, whether moral, social, or political, "must start in the active not the passive will" (235).

His total argument seems willing to surrender the possibility of a divinely impregnated universe in order to make his bald assertion of free will. This chapter in *Orthodoxy* is entitled "The Romance of Orthodoxy" because, through man's free will, the world is suddenly imbued again with the romance and unpredictability that are the major motifs of existential fiction since Dostoyevsky. Like the Russian novelist, Father Brown speaks in awe of man as "the most unreliable machine" whose life will always be filled with challenge, adventure, and mystery.[2] Free will achieves for Chesterton's argument what an Immanent Deity had been allowed to do only for a brief moment.

The last chapter of *Orthodoxy*, which shifts the grounds of the discussion to a historical justification of Christianity, centers on the two incomprehensible and "explosive" events in human history: "Once Heaven came upon the earth with a power or seal called the image of God, whereby man took command of Nature; and once again (when in empire after empire men had been found wanting) Heaven came to save mankind in the awful shape of a man" (249-50). This historical argument is directed, first, at the naturalist-evolutionists who, for a century, had propounded the idea that man's existence was entirely comprehensible in terms of the evolutionary hypothesis, and, second, at the comparative religionists, who habitually argued that Christ was not divine but simply another example of Middle Eastern myth-making. For Chesterton, these theories are both false, for they fail to nullify his "belief that miracles have happened in human history" (258). This belief remains simply a stark assertion by the author which almost becomes obscured in the final flurry of arguments in the concluding pages of *Orthodoxy*. If the historical thesis is almost lost upon the reader, it was not forgotten by its author: he returned to these two historical events seventeen years later and used them as the foundation for a new defense of orthodoxy.

## II The Everlasting Man

*The Everlasting Man* (1925) is divided into two halves: the first, "On the Creature called Man"; the second, "On the

Man called Christ." Its very organization is plainly directed
at fulfilling the schema suggested in the last chapter of *Orthodoxy*, even to the disclaimer that "the view suggested is historical rather than theological." To anyone familiar with the work
of Ernst Cassirer, Alfred North Whitehead, Suzanne Langer,
and a number of other writers about art and symbolism, very
little that appears in the first chapters is new; what is astonishing
is the acumen with which Chesterton, the non-specialist, antici-
pated the findings of linguistic scholars and philosophers in
these areas.

The central theme of the first chapter of *The Everlasting Man*
is now almost a commonplace in academic circles: that man is
not an extension of the animal creation; he is a being unique
because of his powers of symbolization. His uniqueness is first
revealed to himself in those astonishing cave-paintings distrib-
uted throughout Europe and Africa; on the basis of these, one
may make further conjectures about other modes of symbolic
expression in primitive times. Man is undeniably a *saltus naturae*,
a leap of nature, something entirely new and unlike any other
creature; for man knows of no lower animals who, however
crudely, resemble man by painting, sculpting, or exhibiting
any other kind of symbolic expression.[3]

This power of symbolization proves rather conclusively that
man is not a product of evolution but of a "miracle." Chesterton
then recites the other symbolic activities of man—dreams,
laughter, religion, ritual, and even clothing—which recent scholars
of symbolism have offered as refutation of the shallow Positivism
of the nineteenth century (35).

One implication of this data is that progress itself is a myth.
Modern man resembles primitive man much more than primitive
man resembles the beasts; for, according to Chesterton, primitive life, far from being dark, ignorant, and barbarous, had a
considerable amount of "civilization." The cave-paintings are
the primary evidence; and one may assume that primitive man
also succeeded in the creation of language, art, government, and
social organization that still distinguish him from the animal
kingdom. However, all of these achievements were susceptible
of overthrow, of retrogression, of decay; barbarism does not

precede civilization; civilizations lie in layers beside each other throughout history (61-62).

The second quarter of the book again assails the anthropologists and comparative religionists who have dissembled by claiming to have proved that Christianity was simply one more religion—one no better and no less foolish than the other religions throughout the passage of human history. Chesterton complains against the "fallacy by which a false classification is created to swamp a unique thing, when it really is a unique thing" (84). Especially dishonest, to Chesterton, is the scholarly doctrine that Christianity is a product of Greek philosophy and of the Roman polytheism that preceded it. For Chesterton, it was impossible for Classical mythology and Classical philosophy to bring Christianity into existence. Classical polytheism is an example of the imagination that runs riotously free when the "reason does not restrain at all"; and Classical philosophy, best exemplified by Plato, is defined as intellect or rationalism without imagination. Plato's idealism was unearthly, dangerously rarefied, because it was not in contact with the reality of this world. The downfall of the Classical civilization was a direct result of the isolation of philosophers and the common man; the philosophers had a monopoly on the unearthly intellect, and the average man had his wildly imaginative mythology. Because the two were separated, they were unable to modify each other; their powers worked unhindered and unrestrained, and finally succeeded in creating fanciful mythologies and fanciful philosophies (124-25).

The crucial event of the Classical period was Rome's victory over Carthage, which ensured the victory of a somewhat "saner" religion of home, order, and obedience over a religion of child sacrifice and of pessimistic practicality. Rome's victory did not, however, conceal the fact that the old religion was dying—that something of the old vitality had gone out of Pan. Man had extended his powers to the utmost under the Roman gods, but he had found no satisfaction with himself: "it was the strongest thing that was growing weak, while the rest of the world degenerated into barbarism again" (163). Faced with the purposelessness of worldly power, the citizens of Rome turned eagerly for solace to a number of exotic religions from the Middle East.

Apparently, the Roman world was ready for another religion. At this point, Chesterton's defense of Christianity threatens to flounder since it appears historically that Christianity was simply one of those numerous cults which stepped into the vacuum left by the collapse of the Roman pantheon. Chesterton is careful to negate such a conclusion, of course. For him, Christianity is not a logical incident in history but a miraculous replacement of the dying religion by the true religion. It succeeded in establishing itself because it was a higher and truer solution to the religious and psychological needs of Western man.

### III  *"On the Man Called Christ"*

The second half of *The Everlasting Man* is, for the believing Christian, an admirable exposition of the meaning of Christ; but its arguments are open to debate by unbelievers and by those whose faith is somewhat unsteady. In any case, it must be counted as inferior to the first half of the book; for the central issue is the same one Chesterton fumbles in *Orthodoxy*: the problem of the Incarnation. Like many popularizers, Chesterton is at his best when he is describing his personal experiences and extracting implications from them; but when he is forced to deal with erudite philosophical or theological questions in which definition, distinction, detail, and a specialized vocabulary are required, he is apt to sacrifice clarity and thoroughness for immediate impression. The Incarnation is exactly the kind of topic which professional theologians find beset with difficulties; it is little wonder, therefore, that it falls beyond the reach of a popular essayist who must be additionally concerned with matters of space and audience.

Indicative of Chesterton's failure is that, although the ostensible burden of the second half of *The Everlasting Man* is the divinity of Christ, the God-Man, most of the account is in terms of a human drama involving humans with a social and political problem. As Chesterton tells it, the story of the Holy Family is at first a simple bourgeois drama; an unknown family in the Middle East underwent various hardships, a baby was born, and they were visited (without explanation) by shepherds and by the kings of the East. There is nothing in the relation of this drama about an Immaculate Conception or Incarnation; in fact, God is omitted entirely as an active agent (178-80).

The bourgeois tale next shades into a kind of "miracle play" (as in a toy theater) in which Herod, the cruel king of "fairyland" tries to harm the child but is thwarted by an exciting and melodramatic escape of the Family (181). The tale is next converted into "the Christmas story," a timeless piece of literature which had gripped the human imagination and become the core of the Faith. Nowhere yet has the Incarnation been introduced or explained; the reader must be satisfied with the tautology that "No other birth of a god or childhood of a sage seems to us to be Christmas or anything like Christmas" (183).

As Chesterton narrates the story of Christ's youth and maturity, he continues to ignore the intricate problem of Christ's divinity. The reader is informed of His "divine precocity," but he does not know if "divine" is to be taken literally. He is told that Christ's opinions were not those of a man of his time; with this statement, Chesterton begins to retreat to a secular plane, where he argues confidently that Christ "must be put higher in the scale of human beings." Few can disagree about His superiority —even the most agnostic—nor will anyone argue with Chesterton's declaration that Jesus "seems to me to have in a great many ways the note of something superhuman; that is of something human and more than human" (203). Unless these words are to be taken literally (and one suspects that Chesterton is cleverly playing with words), the statement might be stretched to include such men as Gandhi, Buddha, Thomas Jefferson, or Albert Einstein. What the reader is surprised to find revealed to him, in brief, is the Christ of the Humanists or of the Unitarians, and he recalls that as a young boy Chesterton spent his Sunday mornings listening to the Unitarian sermons of Stopford Brooke.

As the story of Christ's life draws to a close, the problem of the Incarnation still remains unanswered. Christ's trial is treated, again surprisingly, as simply a civil case in the decaying Roman Empire. The only "miracle" at this time is that Christ, rather than escaping, stood his ground like any number of Christian martyrs. Faced with the events of the last days of

Christ's life—his betrayal, his agony on the cross, the disappearance of his body, his prayers to God the Father—Chesterton
adopts the position of an unquestioning "O altitudo": "Criticism
is only words about words; and of what use are words about
such words as these?" Such easy assent would have been a
proper, even commendable philosophical position had it emerged
earlier; a reader can be tolerant of the existential leap to faith.
One is uneasy, however, about such a leap being taken at the
end of a tightly reasoned exposition—to have the painful exer-
tions of logic suddenly dismissed with the dictum: "God had
been forsaken of God" (212).

With this leap to faith, however, Chesterton again grasped
the key that had unlocked the various tumblers in *Orthodoxy*.
Everything falls into place. The reader is told that Christianity's
success in the Roman Empire was historically ensured by divine
fiat, or miracle; all the economic, social, and political factors
that may have accounted for the spread of the new religion are
discounted. The book grinds limply to a close with a flurry of
incidental arguments and bland assertions—and none of them is
proved. "If dogma is incredible, it is because it is incredibly
liberal."

Chesterton's central thesis is that the heart of Christianity is
the "doctrine of the divinity of Christ." Yet, in a book which
makes this claim, and which also pretends to be a *defensio fidum*,
the absence of any continuing *discussion* of the central idea
(one understandably does not demand *proof*) is a glaring weakness. For the reader who wants more than entertainment or
reinforcement for his faith, *The Everlasting Man* is a long
syllogism with a faulty major premise.

## IV  St. Thomas Aquinas

Chesterton's brief book on Aquinas (*St. Thomas Aquinas*,
1933) is frequently pointed out as an example of Chesterton's
creative genius. Because of his knowledge of his subject, he
dictated half the book without consulting any authorities what-
soever, looked briefly at some scholarly materials on the subject
carried in by his secretary one day, and then completed his
dictation in a final burst. Although one might expect disastrous

results from such a method, no less a scholar than Etienne Gilson, the foremost authority on St. Thomas Aquinas in the twentieth century, has commented ruefully on Chesterton's *St. Thomas Aquinas*: "I consider it as being without possible comparison the best book ever written on St. Thomas. Nothing short of genius can account for such an achievement. Everybody will no doubt admit that it is a 'clever' book, but the few readers who have spent twenty or thirty years in studying St. Thomas Aquinas, and who, perhaps, have themselves published two or three volumes on the subject, cannot fail to perceive that the so-called 'wit' of Chesterton has put their scholarship to shame. He has guessed all that which they had tried to demonstrate, and he has said all that which they were more or less clumsily attempting to express in academic formulas."[4]

For many readers, Chesterton's *St. Thomas Aquinas* remains his best book. Even if Gilson is somewhat hyberbolic in his praise, one is bound to ask the reasons for Chesterton's fine achievement. While it is probably insufficient to explain the book's success as inevitable, considering the author's affinity for Thomistic philosophy, still one may see that the St. Thomas we find in Chesterton's biography is nothing if he is not "Chestertonian." There are parts of the book, indeed, that read as though Chesterton were writing a self-portrait.

The Aquinas presented by Chesterton is "a large, and heavy, and quiet boy, and phenomenally silent," having woolgathering ways about him; his genius develops early; and, although he comes from a respectable family, he chooses to become a "beggar" in the Dominican order. In school at Paris, he is a tall and bulky figure called "the Dumb Ox" because of his silent, almost stupefied manner. Slowly he makes his way, and Albertus Magnus warns his students that "the Dumb Ox shall bellow so loud that his bellowings will fill the world."

St. Thomas makes his greatest impact, in Chesterton's portrait, not through his theology but through his debates with opposing scholars; he is a contentious man, always ready to enter the lists in defense of the Catholic Church. He is also a "walking wine barrel," a man whose corpulence is a butt to his fellows, and a joke even to himself. When he is not reading—which is rarely—he can be observed in a kind of abstraction, walking rapidly in circles, lost in the airless realm of theology. He descends occasionally to write enough books "to sink a ship or stock a library."

Careless about dress and demeanor and other worldly fripperies, St. Thomas is not a Puritan; in fact, he is a man who enjoys banquets, conviviality, jokes, and pranks. His inner certitude about religious truth permits him to accept the world and its freedom, and it endows him with a childlike innocence. This, too, is as descriptive of Chesterton as it is of Aquinas.

For Chesterton, Aquinas's main appeal lies in his theology, particularly in his efforts to divinize the world. One need not repeat Chesterton's discussion of Thomas's achievement, but one should remark that Chesterton treats the ideas of the Medieval scholar without distortion and with some verve. The central issue of Thomas's theology is the obligation "to treat all this reality as real"—which Chesterton translates as "A is A, a tree is a tree, eggs are eggs."[5] The crux of Thomistic Christianity is the belief "that deity or sanctity has attached to matter or entered the world of the senses"—a statement that is not unrelated to his earlier treatments of Immanence and Incarnation.[6]

The one weakness of *St. Thomas Aquinas* is Chesterton's failure to recognize, or at least emphasize, the far-flung implications of Aquinas's renewal of Aristotelianism in the West. For Chesterton, the Catholic Church always had been and still was a stable point in an unstable world—a restraint, as one critic says, on "all sorts of movements" in history.[7] It had historically restrained the expansion of such innovative forces as empiricism, individualism, and relativism—as Chesterton is willing to admit. On the other hand, in rediscovering Aristotelianism, St. Thomas provided the impetus for the unleashing of these and similar related forces. St. Thomas provided a respectable rationale for empiricism, individualism, and the scientific quest for knowledge in succeeding centuries. In settling one conflict—in favor of a this-worldly realism and common-sense—Aquinas helped foster the Faustian spirit of post-Reformation Europe which Chesterton abominated. The Catholic Church, under the influence of Thomas's thought, ceased to be a source of stability; and it gave birth to those secular forces which Chesterton viewed as the main threat to Western culture.

## V  St. Francis of Assisi

While agreeing with Belloc that everything in Chesterton is "dependent on his religious belief," one can still marvel at his ability, even in such books as *The Everlasting Man* and *St. Thomas Aquinas,* to keep his specifically "Catholic" faith in the background. In a number of books near the end of his life, this Catholicism becomes, however, more aggressive and more unpleasant. More polemical, or at least more personal, these are lesser creations by Chesterton the religious writer: *St. Francis of Assisi* (1923); *The Catholic Church and Conversion* (1927); *The Thing* (1929); *Christendom in Dublin* (1932); and *The Well and the Shallows* (1935).

*St. Francis of Assisi* does not fail (in comparison with *St. Thomas Aquinas*) because it is more polemical but because the subject is less congenial to the critic. St. Thomas was a man of ideas, and Chesterton is a writer whose great strength lies in the analysis and restatement of ideas; St. Francis was a man of mood, and mood is harder to write about, particularly if the author is a man like Chesterton, in whose coarse hands a delicate thing like mood is easily crushed. The biography of St. Francis also lacks the kind of drama that Chesterton could advantageously develop, as he could the kidnapping of St. Thomas by his family, or the incident at the banquet when Thomas pounded the table absentmindedly and thundered, "And *that* will settle the Manichees." After St. Francis had abandoned his social position for the life of a friar, much of the drama in his life was over; and the biographer of St. Francis must then content himself with handling minor incidents, the delicate relationships between men, and above all the interior life of the soul. One must admit that Chesterton strives to do so, but the result is a rather saccharine "appreciation" that lacks sufficient intellectual analysis of Francis and his movement.

## VI  The Catholic Church and Conversion

*The Catholic Church and Conversion* (1927) attempts to define Catholicism from the point of view of a convert and then to describe the process by which the initiate approaches the Church. The book opens with a wordy defense of the Catholic

Church against modern anti-clericalism and the literature of
the "Maria Monk school" (lubricious priests, bastard-bearing
nuns, and bishops bent on rape). The author then attempts to
explicate "the way of the soul" to the bosom of the Church.
Before he begins, however, he takes care to criticize the shallow
conversion which occurred so frequently in the "Decadent movement" of the nineties. At that time, a number of esthetic personalities like Pater, Beardsley, and Wilde had been drawn to the
Catholic Church simply on the basis of the numerous appeals
to the senses made during the ritual—the odor of incense, the
costuming of the priests, the music, and the sculptures and
paintings in the interior.

Chesterton, who resists such sensualism, opposes to it a conversion process that is entirely intellectual. At the start, the novice
lives with an easy impartiality to the ideas of Catholicism (similar to Carlyle's "Center of Indifference"); in the second stage,
he is driven to an intense and earnest study of Church doctrine;
in the third stage, he easily gravitates to the Church. The
crucial stage, of course, is the second, during which the seeker
studies not just the Catholic faith but divests himself of past
errors by redefining words and terms that have otherwise been
"spoiled" or neglected in a secularist society.[8] For Chesterton,
then, conversion is an intellectual act that requires the novice
to "think harder than he has ever thought in his life." And this
view is Chesterton's explicit rebuttal of the Decadent idea of
"conversion by beautiful catastrophe."[9]

On the larger problem of the "truth" of the Catholic faith,
Chesterton is less convincing. Again he repeats the argument of
*Orthodoxy* and *The Everlasting Man*: that the Church, since it
is always being attacked by opposite extremes, must be reposing
at some central position, "the Truth"—and the fallacy of this
logic has been discussed. Equally faulty is Chesterton's thesis
that the Calvinists, Quakers, Bolsheviks, Moslems—all the Protestant sects and all heresies—are Catholics manqués, each of
them having taken some single doctrine of the central "Truth"
and distorted it through some overemphasis. Catholicism may
be viewed as a huge continent, out of which has been chipped
the smaller, inferior fragments one sees all around. Chesterton
is, however, less than convincing in arguing that Catholicism

"contains" all the Protestant sects and heresies.[10] For example, Catholicism in no meaningful way "contains" the doctrines of Spiritualism, Christian Science, or Islam. Calvinism may be implicit in Catholic doctrine, as a seed may be contained in a mature fruit; this fact does not prove that the developed fruit is the same as, or inferior to, the seed.

## VII   *Later Polemics*

What is new in *The Catholic Church and Conversion* is a note of militancy, of anti-Protestantism, that increases in Chesterton's later books. If there is any change in Chesterton's personality or thought (and there has been some discussion on this point), it is certainly in the fact that the good humor, tolerance, and refreshing innocence of the early Chesterton is replaced by a more strident and aggressive religiosity. Perhaps this new note developed from his increasing awareness of his failure to change his world and from a renewed desire to reach some audience— even if in a high pitched voice.

This stridency reaches its peak in the late 1920's and early 1930's in the ill-named *The Thing, Christendom in Dublin,* and *The Well and the Shallows.* The tone of *The Thing* is established by the thesis that "The Thing" (The Church) is "either attacked or defended; and he that is not against it is for it."[11] The line has been drawn, and the positions are more rigid than they have ever been. The book is an unceasing eulogy of the Catholic Church, which is described as the sole protector of reason and as the only true philosophy. Protestantism is defined as a relapse into barbarism: the Reformation in England, for example, was carried out by capitalists acting in "a stampede of brutal luxury and pride with a vulgar howl of hot-gospelling for an excuse, a riot of thieves and looters with a few foaming and gibbering Manichees, the dirty ape of the ascetic, conspiring with the devil to destroy the world" (231).

The style of this passage (not atypical of the whole book) is a pathetic indication that the genial Chesterton is no longer in command. In arguing the need for the immediate conversion of all the Protestants in England, he says that "conversion is the beginning of an active, fruitful, progressive, and even adventurous life of the intellect" (217). *The Thing* reveals, however, that the intellect of at least one convert has become decidedly retrogressive and unadventurous.

The tone is worse in *The Well and the Shallows*, an *omnium gatherum* of essays from several sources; but they are important because they are among the last things Chesterton wrote. All the humor is gone, and humor was often the only element that buoyed up Chesterton's ideas or prejudices. An essay on "The Surrender upon Sex" is typical in its uncompromising Catholicism ("the well") and its abuse of Protestantism—divorce, birth "prevention," sex, and human nature in general. The whole world of "the shallows" is a whirl of malicious enemies—one no longer distinguishable to a man who once prized the quality of discreteness in life.

The main thesis of *The Well and the Shallows* is that one is either a Catholic or a person who stands among the millions of evildoers of this world. The line is firmly drawn by an author who has discovered "the fundamental truth of the modern world": that "there are no Fascists; there are no Socialists; there are no Liberals; there are no Parliamentarians. There is the one supremely inspiring and irritating institution in the world; and there are its enemies" (64). This is Manicheism pure and simple; for there are no longer any answers, either of a secular or religious nature; divine grace is shut off from the numberless enemies, and even secular solutions like Distributism seem to be absolute folly.

As for himself, Chesterton complacently fondles the reassuring thought that "I had chosen well." Now he can wait for some Armageddon: "I should have liked the ordinary, old fashioned, obstinate people, who still stick to the notion of some connection between themselves and their own babies, to rise and bash in the heads of the inhuman prigs whose ideal is a sort of prophetic infanticide. . . . should prefer the Intellectuals to be slaughtered by what may be called the Morals" (92). Truth exclusively identified with Catholic dogma, merciless war advocated against all heretics, and Armageddon defined as the complete eradication of the enemies of the Catholic Church—such is the mood of the later years. Chesterton had progressed some distance from the jovial biographies of Browning and Dickens, the optimistic propaganda for Distributism, or the tolerant latitudinarianism of *Orthodoxy*.

## VIII  *Chesterton As Defender of the Faith*

If one were forced to characterize Chesterton in a few words, it would be no great misrepresentation to say that he was a champion of religion against the combined forces of secularism, science, and Positivism. Like his Victorian predecessors, he was convinced "that a religious war is raging under the surface, which would be much better if it were raging on the surface."[12] He rejects the fruits of science because they fail to provide society with ends, standards, or values. Looking at the factories, mills, shipyards, and belching furnaces of Belfast, he turned to his boastful guide and asked, "Have you ever asked what all this is for?[13] The question might be considered a touchstone for Chesterton's thought.

With science in general, with such "pseudo-sciences" as psychology and evolution, he also rejected such modern secular "religions" as Couéism, Communism, and Humanism: "The secular ideals of humanity fossilize very fast, and nothing but religion ever remains."[14] To such secular religions he opposes legends, superstitions, belief in witchcraft and household gods, and, always, the return to Christianity. For the pride of the modern secular state, he prescribes a belief in Original Sin: "Humanism may try to pick up the pieces; but can it stick them together? Where is the cement which made religion corporate and popular, which can prevent it falling to pieces in a debris of individualistic tastes and decrees?"[15]

Two questions arise in connection with Chesterton's religious beliefs. The first is whether the Catholic Chesterton—even the irately polemical one—was inherent in the young man. The answer must be affirmative, if one can exclude the young man of the Notebooks, the young Socialist-atheist of the very brief Slade School period. To his friends, nothing became Chesterton so much as his conversion, for it came as no surprise. To the general public, the only surprise was that Chesterton, it was discovered, had not been what he had seemed to be for so many years. One concludes again with Chesterton and with a number of critics that there was no important change or development of ideas in his thought.

As for the second question about how effective Chesterton was as a Catholic apologist, one must conclude that his reputation as a "Catholic writer"—mistakenly promoted by intense Catholics—repels many readers who would profit by reading him. His fame as a "doctor of the Church" has served primarily to prevent his works from gaining the attention they richly deserve. In judging his religious writings, it would be facile to dismiss Chesterton as "only a popularizer." His analysis of philosophical and religious problems is only too frequently done with a large brush. When the intellectual argument becomes complex and intricate, Chesterton's essays simplify; they lack the exquisite distinctions, the interlocking argument, the careful definitions that are annoying but indispensable in philosophical and theological writing.

Nevertheless, there is much to be said for such simplification which presents the broad outlines of things and outlines the central issues of philosophy and theology to a large audience. Every culture needs someone to discern the central issues—to see the broad philosophical concepts through the tangle of subtle and sometimes trivial explication that accretes around them; and rarely does Chesterton fail to illuminate for his readers what the main forms and outlines of thought are. Too often, however, Chesterton, when faced with complex intellectual problems and when hampered by the requirements of the brief essay, pretends to explain and does not; he appears to be complete, but he is really oversimplifying. And very frequently he retreats to the Quietism of the mystic, an "O altitudo" that is incongruous in the context of a journalistic essay meant to explain and clarify for a broad audience.

Chesterton's works have their real justification in the vitality of the author's personality which animates them. One cannot think of another writer with his capacity of *explaining* by means of vivid examples, comparisons, and analogies: they bring alive for the common reader the problems of philosophy and religion that otherwise would have remained interred in the dust of university and seminary libraries. Perhaps one should say that in these philosophical and religious writings Chesterton was something of an artist and that he could not be simply a philosopher or theologian or even propagandist. This impulse to be more than expositor, to create something artistically original, is manifested also in the large number of novels, stories, and poems written throughout his life; for many of these contain the same themes found in his social and philosophical works.

# CHAPTER 6

## Detectives and Apocalypses

DESCRIBING the fiction of the 1890's, one critic states that "the sane tradition of English fiction by which a delicate balance was maintained between realism and romance rarely broke down."[1] That delicate balance was upset, of course, with the new century when it became obvious that fiction-writers had gravitated into two camps: that of the Realists and Naturalists—Americans like Frank Norris and Theodore Dreiser, English writers like Arnold Bennett, John Galsworthy, Somerset Maugham, and young James Joyce; and a smaller group of "romancers" like Rudyard Kipling, H. G. Wells, James Barrie, William Butler Yeats, and Chesterton himself.

As has been observed, Chesterton the critic had opted against "the vulgarity that is called realism," wielding his prejudice most effectively against those Realists who were always condemning Dickens for his "melodramas" and "caricatures."[2] Chesterton's critical animus against "realism" is of a piece with the "anti-realism" of his fiction. The word "fiction" is used deliberately because he did not write "novels" so much as "romances" or "fictions": he is more safely located in the tradition of Sir Walter Scott than in that of Jane Austen. In fact, Chesterton's romances resist all the allurements of the modern novel (inherited largely from Jane Austen): the bourgeois ambience, the cool efficiency of style, the psychological interest, and the materialistic value system.

Chesterton's romances are not "pure" romances; they are combined with what Northrop Frye calls "anatomies"—fictions which are essentially written for purposes of presenting and analyzing ideas. Once again one detects in Chesterton that sheer love of ideas—even above his love of humans—that sensation of a pulsing vitality in all ideas and concepts. His life was spent pouring his ideas into his weekly columns, letters to editors,

120

book-length studies, debates with Socialists and atheists, and lectures to generally enchanted audiences. His seventeen volumes of fiction (more than Dickens wrote) may be considered as an important extension of this intellectual or propagandistic activity.

Although these romance-anatomies have their defenders—the small coterie of Chestertonians—they remain generally unread and unmentioned by historians of the novel. The probable source of this critical disapproval is not their didacticism (which is, in spite of accepted tradition, epidemic in the modern novel) but Chesterton's candor about it. Like Anthony Trollope before him, Chesterton scorned the tidiness of modern critical taste; and, as has been seen, he confessed to believing in the "usefulness" of fiction. He firmly held to the idea that "you cannot tell a story without the idea of pursuing a purpose and sticking to a point."[3]

The concentration on "purpose" and "point" and the cavalier use of the word "story" (instead of the critically more fashionable "plot") suggest something of his insouciance about the esthetics of fiction—and also explain a certain narrowness of range in his own fictions. In matters of plotting, for example, Chesterton's romances are organized around only two types of *mythos*: that of the detective questing for the truth and that of an Armageddon involving the struggle of some hero (usually with a small band of followers) against an overwhelmingly superior enemy. The two myths, alternating through his fictions and sometimes appearing together, undoubtedly reflect Chesterton's self-concept—his vision of his struggle in modern life, his desire to uncover the truth, and his isolation in the important controversies of his age.

## I  Father Brown

For Chesterton, who was himself addicted to reading detective stories, this popular genre was not merely escapist amusement for the masses but a powerful vehicle for transmitting the moral, religious, and political ideals of society. Such stories, "the centre of a million flaming imaginations," were much more important than the so-called "literary masterpieces"—and especially the more recent ones that are merely "books recommending profligacy and pessimism." To Chesterton, the universal popularity of the detective story proves an important point: "The simple need for some world in which fictitious persons play an unhampered part is infinitely deeper and older than the rules of good art, and much more important."[4] Thus, Chesterton found both philosophical and pragmatic reasons for resorting to the detective mode. In five Father Brown collections (or a total of 51 stories) and five other books in which crime detection is the central *mythos*, he revealed how easily he could work with the mode.

The Father Brown stories, appearing from 1910 to 1935 in such journals as *Storyteller* and *Pall Mall Magazine*, are by far the most popular and most widely known works that Chesterton ever wrote. They were eventually collected into five books: *The Innocence of Father Brown* (1911); *The Wisdom of Father Brown* (1914); *The Incredulity of Father Brown* (1926); *The Secret of Father Brown* (1927); and *The Scandal of Father Brown* (1935). The success and popularity of the Father Brown stories (they are still widely reprinted today) probably derive from their basis in Chesterton's experience. The hero of the stories, a short, squat, helpless-appearing Catholic priest, was based on an actual priest, Father (later Monsignor) John O'Connor, a lifelong friend of Chesterton who received the author into the Catholic faith.

The original inspirations for the stories were Chesterton's discovery of Father O'Connor's profound knowledge of the depths of human depravity, and a conversation at a dinner party during which two brash Cambridge students commented sarcastically about the naïveté of modern Christian priests.[5] Chesterton was struck by the paradox of an outwardly innocent appearance (his hero's "blank expression like an idiot's" also recalls Mr. Pickwick) and his deep understanding of sin and evil. A large part of the lasting charm of these stories is born in the striking contrast between the childlike hero and the darkly sinful situations in which he is placed.

It is difficult to detect (as some critics claim to do) any important change in the Father Brown stories as Chesterton grew older. Like any successful journeyman writer, he realized that it was unwise to change a profitable formula that one had hit upon; therefore, the general format of the stories is fairly consistent. The setting is usually recherché: a mansion, a resort, a plush hotel, or a restaurant. As though the lower-classes are immune to scandal or violence, the main characters are usually drawn from the aristocracy, the upper middle-class, or the hangers-on of either—intelligentsia, professional men, high civil servants, or artists. Mixed with these characters is a touch of the exotic in the form of eccentrics, mystics, seers, magicians, cult-worshippers, fakirs, or sinister-looking distant relatives.

A familiar formula appears: the early suspicions fall on one of the exotics, but the suspect proves to be innocent while one of his more respectable friends is revealed to be the culprit. The range of situations in which this formula is expressed is fairly narrow; frequently, it is a variation of the "purloined letter" motif (a crime is committed, and the clues somehow remain unseen although in plain view) or the "closed room" situation (some crime is committed, and the criminal escapes from an inescapable situation).

Chesterton's detective makes a complete break with Edgar Allan Poe's Dupin and with A. Conan Doyle's Sherlock Holmes "ratiocinative" tradition of the detective story. Father Brown loses no opportunity to disparage Holmes, whom he ridicules for living in a lonely house with his "opium and acrostics."[6] Father Brown's detective pursuits are truly Chestertonian in that they shun the techniques of science and the undiluted rational powers of man. "Mere facts are commonplace," says Father Brown, who prefers intuition of the truth, which depends on a deep knowledge of the human heart instead of methodical observation. "I go by a man's eyes and voice, don't you know, and whether his family seems happy, and by what subjects he chooses and avoids."[7] In a startling echo of Blake, Father Brown attributes his success to the fact that "I am a man and therefore have all devils in my heart."[8]

But Chesterton and his hero are not disciples of Freud. Father Brown rejects "All this deeper psychology" as "improbable." His psychology is Aristotelian, or Catholic, resting on the assumption that human psychology is very often "simpler than you understand."[9] A pleasant young man who had been disinherited can be expected to do anything, even commit murder; a lustful woman when linked to an older husband will very likely attempt to gain her freedom; pride can so infect a man that he will commit suicide in order to incriminate a man who has insulted him.

In addition to this knowledge of the "human heart," Chesterton's detective is guided by certain theological truths. He automatically suspects anyone who "philosophizes along those lines of orientalism and recurrence and reincarnation."[10] In a frequently anthologized story, "The Blue Cross," he captures the arch-criminal Flambeau (later to become Father Brown's good friend and a detective), when Flambeau, disguised as a priest, argues the heresy that reason is completely untrustworthy.[11] Nor does Chesterton always succeed at keeping his social and political biases out of his stories: Father Brown's favorite rule of thumb is that, although all men are potential sinners and criminals, one human type that "tends at times to be more utterly godless than another" is the "brutal sort of business man."[12]

Father Brown's techniques—or non-techniques—too often result in a kind of "miraculous insight," as one critic asserts, that makes the game hardly worth playing after a while. One accepts, as one must of all detectives, the donnée of the hero's presence at the scene of the crime. What is tedious is the ease with which the hero solves his cases on the basis of intuition. The recurrent formula soon becomes wearisome: a number of suspects are paraded before the reader, clues are given or withheld, and Father Brown after some discussion announces that he knows— and has always known—the identity of the criminal. The particular psychological insight or theological maxim is then displayed for the reader's edification, and the story ends.

The preachments, the Gothic coloration of setting and character, and the swift rendering of atmosphere, have served to make Chesterton one of the most popular writers of detective fiction in the twentieth century and at one time the president of the Detective Club—a post which he filled with predictable seriousness. However, these stories are important parts of his total work only for those who are addicted to the genre. For most readers, only the unusual portrait of Father Brown—perhaps Chesterton's only fully developed fictional creation—can be of lasting interest. It is doubtful that even Chesterton would have contended that these fifty-one stories are among his finest achievements.

## II   *Other Detective Fictions*

The didacticism of the Father Brown stories is relatively restrained in comparison with several other detective fictions which seem to preach the Chestertonian doctrine unremittingly. *The Man Who Knew Too Much* (1922) displays, against the postwar background, a hero whose hobby is the "phenomena of phosphorescence," or, less cutely, the political corruption of the modern state. The criminals prove to be estimable social figures such as a Prime Minister who improbably strangles a financier (decidedly Jewish) because he is, equally improbably, a dictator of English foreign policy. Horne Fisher's dark night of the soul occurs when he discovers that his own family has rigged an election against him in favor of a Disraeli-like "foreign vermin" who has "arranged the Egyptian Loan and Lord knows what else." In a final Armageddon, the hero dies leading an army against a horde of Chinese coolies imported by "foreign interests" to compete with the English peasantry in the labor market.

The stories of *The Man Who Knew Too Much* are a useful litmus indicator of Chesterton's gloom in the years after the war, a despair which one may also observe in such works as *Fancies versus Fads*, written at the same time. The death of the hero may be the author's image of his own role as a prophet without honor who must die eventually in defense of his country's most cherished traditions.

Gabriel Gale, the hero of *The Poet and the Lunatics* (1929) continues Horne Fisher's struggles on more philosophical ground: Gale is a defender of feeling, intuition, the religious spirit, who is soon oppressed by various "usurers" and Semitic doctors. When they threaten to throw him into a lunatic asylum, one of his "mad" friends holds these scientists and modernists at bay with a gun just long enough for Gale to escape to his small freehold. There he can indulge himself endlessly by painting satiric portraits of his enemies, certain that on his own property the state cannot intervene. The idyllic ending may be Chesterton's own gratuitous dream projection of a life dedicated to innocent art without the fear of being persecuted by a Prussianized society.

Least impressive of Chesterton's fictions are the contrived *Four Faultless Felons* (1930) and the utterly charmless *The Paradoxes of Mr. Pond* (1937). The first centers on the gimmickry of a "Club of Misunderstood Men," who are publicly scorned for crimes and pecadilloes which are secretly committed for the greater glory of God; thus one clubman plays the role of fastidious gourmand before the eyes of a hostile society, but secretly is an ascetic who detests the role—preferring to bear it as a kind of cross. In the second book, there are even more tedious mystifications and situations, presided over by a protagonist, Mr. Pond, who is wooden beyond belief despite a promising fish-like appearance. One may add that the liveliest writing in both books appears when Chesterton is inveighing against modern liberalism, science, the Jewish influence on England, and materialism.

### III   The Napoleon of Notting Hill

More consequential than Chesterton's detective fictions, including the Father Brown stories, are his romances, all of which take the form of apocalyptic myths. In each of them a stalwart hero and a group of followers confront the forces of evil in some grand, climactic struggle. Of these, *The Napoleon of Notting Hill* (1904) must be ranked supreme, and may be the most quintessentially Chestertonian romance. He himself tended to deprecate this achievement in later years, not because his views had changed but because he thought the book was incomplete in its social vision. Nevertheless, he also had a lasting affection (as we can observe in his *Autobiography* and elsewhere) for what he modestly called a "fortunately forgotten book."[13]

*The Napoleon of Notting Hill* sprang naturally out of the climate of the Boer War, the main lesson of which, its author said, was "that a small nation had a positive value of its own."[14] In an interview, he related how his anti-imperialistic bias had crystallized during a walk through a quaint section of London, possibly Notting Hill itself:

There is such a thing as a dilated, or swelled head. But the typical case of a creature who dilated equally all round is that of the imperially-minded frog who wanted to be a bull, and dilated until he burst. . . . In that half second of time, gazing with rapt admiration at the row of little shops, nobly flanked by a small pub and a small church, I discovered that not only was I against the plutocrats, I was against the idealists. In the comparatively crystalline air of that romantic village I heard the clear call of a trumpet. And, once for all, I drew my sword—purchased in the old curiosity shop—in defence of Notting Hill.[15]

More than the Boer War and Chamberlain's Imperialism was troubling Chesterton at the time. In the *Autobiography* he relates that his general malaise at the time—a kind of "madness"— led him "in the direction of some vague and visionary revolt against the prosaic flatness of nineteenth century city and civili- zation . . . the feeling that those imprisoned in these inhuman outlines were human beings; that it was a bad thing that living souls should be thus feebly and crudely represented by houses like ill-drawn diagrams of Euclid, or streets and railways like dingy sections of machinery" (132). The intellectual impetus behind *The Napoleon*, then, is the Ruskinian esthetic—that human ills derive partly from an ugly environment and vice versa.

The book opens with a kind of anti-Utopia of 1984: a servile England of the future is populated mainly by robot-like func- tionaries, all uniformed in bowlers and black suits, and armed with umbrellas. "Everything in that age had become mechani- cal." The government runs smoothly not because the citizens love it but because they have lost their faith in revolution; it is a "dull popular despotism without illusion." The only element of chance or adventure—perhaps reflecting Chesterton's belief that no system can be completely rational—is that the king is chosen periodically by lot; the system has worked so well in the past that no one expects that it will ever blunder.

The plot begins when the system selects as the next king a government functionary named Auberon Quin, who is inexpli- cably unlike his fellow clerks. A kind of early Dadaist, he is given to telling pointless stories, standing on his head on the sidewalk, and bearing like a grail the accumulated nonsense of the human race. (Said to be based on Max Beerbohm, Auberon Quin's name is significant: the Auberon probably alludes to the king of the fairies, and the Quin may be a reference to the madcap eighteenth-century English actor.) What is unexplained is how Quin's zaniness and imaginative powers could have survived the crushing forces of the Orwellian Superstate that Chesterton describes.

As soon as Quin is crowned, he begins to impose his mad vision on his materialistic polity. His main goal is to reestablish the past, particularly the local pride that sections of London once had; he revives Medieval liveries, rituals, local holidays, costumes, and heraldry. The pragmatic and mechanical are displaced by the beauty of the ritualistic; highway building and urban development are brought to a halt.

Quin's program accelerates with the appearance of a lunatic figure named Adam Wayne, who enthusiastically embraces the gospel of Medieval smallness. As a man of pure feeling, he deplores the world's becoming "more and more modern... practical... bustling and rational." Better than Quin he perceives that the progressive achievements of modern society have had their psychological effects: "What a farce is this modern liberality. Freedom of speech means practically in our modern civilization that we must only talk about unimportant things. We must not talk about religion for that is illiberal.... It cannot last. Something must break this strange indifference, this strange dreamy egoism, this strange loneliness of millions in a crowd. Something must break it. Why should it not be you and I?"[16]

With Quin's approval, Wayne pledges his life to implementing Quin's plans. The battle is joined when he prevents the plutocrats from levelling Notting Hill in order to build a railroad. In the colorful battles that follow, Adam Wayne's zeal enables him to rout the forces of materialism and modernism. The Armageddon occurs in the "Battle of the Lamps," so-called because Wayne defeats his enemies in pitch darkness by snuffing out the man-made street lamps which the makers thought were infallible. With this success, the Medieval cause of the two heroes spreads rapidly through England; localities are redeemed from their long sleep of modernism; the old England dreamed of by Carlyle, Ruskin, and Morris is suddenly revived.

In *The Coloured Lands,* Chesterton reminisced about the books of his youth, saying that they were "mostly about the beauty and necessity of wonder" (157). *The Napoleon of Notting Hill* shows Chesterton as a kind of Pre-Raphaelite, for he preaches the esthetic doctrine of strangeness and beauty as antidotes for the progress of the material world. What is missing on Notting Hill is an interest in religion; cathedrals exist, but only as part of the local color. *The Napoleon of Notting Hill* is Chesterton's dream vision, a catharsis of the frustrations he felt in the early years of the century, but the novel still lacks a religious center because he himself had not settled into a religious commitment.

Chesterton's next piece of fiction *The Club of Queer Trades* (1905) continues the theme of "the beauty and necessity of wonder," albeit on a much more didactic level. The fantasy of a Medieval society in the twentieth century is abandoned for a mechanical plot device: an "Adventure and Romance Agency" which hires itself out to bring romance into the lives of those bored by mechanical routine. The Agency sends out "threatening letters," arranges for "secret meetings" and "close escapes," brings together "mysterious strangers," and so on. Chesterton's own psychological needs are perhaps revealed in the Agency's boast that it provides the customer "his childhood, that godlike time when we can act stories, be our own heroes, and at the same instance dance and dream."[17]

## IV  The Man Who Was Thursday

If one wishes to date the beginning of Chesterton's commitment to religion as an answer to the problems of modern man, it is safe to point to 1908, the year of both *Orthodoxy* and *The Man Who Was Thursday*. In a later essay, he said that the novel was written "in the middle of a thick London fog of positive pessimism and materialism,"[18] and the dedication to E. C. Bentley speaks of that era when

> A cloud was on the mind of men, and wailing went the weather,
> Yea, a sick cloud upon the soul when we were boys together.[19]

The subtitle *A Nightmare,* underscores one of its features (and also relates it to almost all his other romances).[20] In the nightmare the hero, a young poet named Syme, hears of a Super-Council of Anarchists bent on the destruction of society, law, and religion. When Syme vows to fight this monstrous conspiracy, he joins a chapter of detectives whose sole purpose is to track down and destroy the anarchists. By accident, he is then introduced into a meeting of the Council of Seven Days, the very Anarchist Super-Council he has been seeking. The strange name is derived from the fact that its seven members carry the names of the days: the leader of the Council is a large, jovial, almost Falstaffian figure named Sunday; and he is strangely out of place, thinks Syme, at a meeting of such a sinister group. When Syme boldly asks to be made the replacement for a recently deceased member, Thursday, he is welcomed into the group.

Once inside the group, the hero has misgivings; he seems alone, cut off from all safety, surrounded by evil. In a rapid succession of shocking episodes, each of the others on the Council is revealed to be a detective enlisted in the same agency to fight the Anarchist Council; and each has been sworn in by the same large, hidden figure in a dark room. Although appearing to be Anarchists, they are really members of the police; they have been both Good and Evil, legal and illegal.

In a final fantastic sequence, the gross but harmless figure Sunday flies in a balloon to his estate, pursued all the way by his mystified lieutenants. Sunday, of course, proves to have two sides: he is Chief Anarchist and Chief of Detectives; he is the gay trickster; he is anarchic; he defies the codes of society; he is absent-minded and innocent; he is always well-meaning. (Chesterton was willing to admit that there was a touch of self-portraiture in Sunday.)[21]

Sunday is like nature itself, or the universe; he is, indeed, Pan—the whole world, all of life. He shows that while life may appear to be dark, nasty, and brutish from one angle, from another and more informed point of view, it appears to be good. It is a matter of an individual's choosing; in having chosen to enlist in the fight against evil and nihilism, the detectives have transformed Sunday into what he really is. Their acceptance of life brings them into harmony with it; they find themselves accepted and loved by Sunday, who tells them at his mansion that they can now find "pleasure in everything." Their only argument now is with one another: each is sure that Sunday's estate is modeled on the scenes of his own youth. What they have gained with their understanding of Sunday is the innocent vision of youth which Chesterton always extolled.

*The Man Who Was Thursday* still presents problems for the critics since it seems to be teaching the highly unChestertonian message that there is no evil, that evil is an illusion, that things are not what they seem. Recognizing the ambiguity, Chesterton later explained, "I was not then considering whether anything is really evil, but whether everything is really evil; and in relation to the latter nightmare it does still seem to be relevant to say that nightmares are not true."[22] The operative word here is "everything"; the problem is not the relativity of values but the discovery that—as the Dedication emphasizes—one might take a small step in finding *some* thing good in spite of the pessimism and gloom of the Edwardian period.

Even while writing, though, Chesterton must have sensed the shaky philosophical ground upon which he stood. In the last scene, while a general Dickensian reconciliation is occurring at a magnificently described masked ball, a Satanic figure steps forward to challenge Sunday again. The relativistic conflict of most of the book makes way for pure Manicheism. "Satan" demands to know the meaning of the masquerade that Sunday has arranged. Why were the detective-anarchists forced in ignorance to play two roles at once? Why were they not granted the meaning of the game without the mummery, the deceit, the struggle, the final embarrassment?

The answer that Sunday gives is straight out of Browning's "Rabbi Ben Ezra." The detectives, Sunday informs everybody, were made to fight "evil," or think they were fighting "evil," "so that each thing that obeys law may have the glory and isolation of the anarchist. So that each man fighting for order may be as brave and good a man as the dynamiter." The struggle against evil, the very sense of an evil to be overcome—has endowed the detectives with the moral virtue spoken of by Rabbi Ben Ezra, who teaches that evil is "Machinery just meant/ To give thy soul its bent."

Chesterton, however, moves beyond Browning's concept of evil. The Tempter still confronts Sunday with piercing questions; he accuses Sunday of not having suffered the fear and doubt felt by his lieutenants during their dark agony. Sunday painfully replies, in the words of Christ, "Can ye drink of the cup that I drink of?" As the book ends, Syme's nightmare is shattered by this question, which stands as a beacon now for the hero, for Chesterton, and for the reader. *The Man Who Was Thursday* is a milestone in Chesterton's progress from the secular-Medieval fantasies of *The Napoleon of Notting Hill* to the complete acceptance of Christian mystery and duty. Serenity and hope, if it can be found at all, will come to the individual who is willing to accept the burden of the Cross.

## V   The Ball and the Cross

The religious strain is more accentuated in Chesterton's next romance, *The Ball and the Cross* (U.S., 1909; England, 1910). The title alludes to the ornaments on the dome of St. Paul's cathedral in London; the ball represents, to Chesterton, the world, its rationalism, its completeness and self-sufficiency; the cross symbolizes the paradoxical religion toward which mankind strives. In a prefatory chapter, we are shown the archfiend Lucifer, in a flying machine, depositing an eccentric monk from an unnamed Balkan country on the dome of St. Paul's. The monk must make the dangerous descent from the ball and cross to the safety of the ground. The main effect of this preamble is to establish the reality of two forces, Good and Evil, which had been left rather ambiguous in *The Man Who Was Thursday*.

The main plot involves a conflict between two young men, John Turnbull, a liberal publisher of an unpopular newspaper "The Atheist," and a young Scottish Catholic named Evan Mac-Ian. They are attempting to fight a duel on the question of the truth of the Virgin Mary. Everywhere they meet with stupefied indifference (the materialistic and pragmatic mind cannot comprehend the purpose of such a quarrel) or the formal opposition of the government. Most of the book is devoted to their futile attempts to fight the duel ("We must kill each other—or convert each other"), and the means by which their attempts are thwarted by well-meaning secularists or by malicious powers of organized society.

Eventually, they find themselves prisoners in an insane asylum—Chesterton's preeminent symbol of modern society. The prisoners are not just MacIan and Turnbull, but all those who take the quarrel seriously; free to roam around outside are those loyal to a secular world of Science and Efficiency. In such a milieu, the two antagonists (like those in *Thursday*) naturally discover that they have much in common and are quickly reconciled. They also discover that a third force—the force of modern science, of power divorced from morality—is determined to destroy them. Turnbull, the modern liberal, is closer to MacIan than either of them had supposed; they are both moralists concerned with "ends." Turnbull's desire for power has always been for the purpose of aiding humanity, and both are fighting Chesterton's *bête noire*, Prussianism, the dehumanized use of human beings. (In "Letters to an Old Garibaldian," 1915, Chesterton interpreted World War I as a union of Catholic Italy and Liberal England—otherwise quite different—against the Prussian hordes.) Both the Catholic and Liberal are Kantians, determined to treat the individual as an end in himself, not as a means to an end.

Chesterton's alarm is generated by the endless aggrandizement of science. In a dream, Turnbull sees that his own methodology of rationalism leads nowhere since it cannot reveal if man has a soul; and, if Turnbull has no soul, the scientists who hold him captive will have little reason to spare him. Turnbull resigns his atheistic rationalism (significantly because of this irrational dream) and adopts an attitude of active love and respect for his fellow man. Each of the two heroes has been guided by some teleology, and they have been considered "mad" by a world that no longer has a teleological viewpoint. Chesterton makes clear that their teleologies are as yet incomplete; Turnbull's humanism is admirable but has no solid basis; MacIan's religious fervor, though well-meaning, is a selfish faith divorced from reason. Symbolically, they occupy cells "B" and "C" in the insane asylum.

The resident of cell "A" is the Balkan monk of the Preface, who is more feared by the authorities because he combines the humanism of Turnbull and the religious faith of MacIan without destroying either. He is, in a sense, a Hegelian synthesis of these two opponents and another version of Sunday in *The Man Who Was Thursday*. In a crucial scene, Turnbull and MacIan enter the cell to see the monk; he is, at the same time, both ancient yet youthful, venerable and childlike; gloomy and weighted with knowledge, yet gay, even comic; living meagerly but still radiating an inner strength; dwarfish, but gigantic in the magnetic influence he exerts. Like Sunday, he is a reconciliation of these opposites—the peace that passeth understanding, the rare mystery of self-sacrifice to faith. His only words to the heroes, as he points to a nail-like projection in the wall, is a barely intelligible, "Spike is best"—again the recommendation of Christian suffering and martyrdom.

In the final scene, the monk miraculously leads all the prisoners safely through the fire which levels the asylum. The modern headquarters of amoral science is razed by the peasants who live nearby and who represent Chesterton's continual hope for the world. The devil-doctor (now plainly identified as Lucifer) escapes in his airplane, and Turnbull and MacIan fall to their knees in worshipful incomprehension of the miracles wrought by the monk.

*The Ball and the Cross* is an advance over *The Man Who Was Thursday* not as a work of art but as a religious statement that depicts Chesterton's growing convictions about Christianity. The ambiguities of *The Man Who Was Thursday* are no longer in evidence: Evil is present and active throughout the book, first as an actual character in the Preface, then as the doctor of the asylum; Good is clearly defined by the character of the monk. Because of this strong polarization of forces, the less carefully drawn characters, and the more overt themes, this romance is a lesser esthetic achievement.

## VI  Manalive

*Manalive* (1912) returns somewhat unexpectedly to the lessons of *The Club of Queer Trades*—and primarily to the theme of modern man's need for adventure and romance. The decline of Chesterton's artistic powers is somewhat indicated by the name of his hero: Innocent Smith. Like the clients of the "Adventure and Romance Agency," Innocent renews romance and excitement in his own life by such stratagems as sneaking into his own house like a burglar, eloping with his wife repeatedly in order to retain the romance in their marriage, and walking around the earth to discover how good his home is. For others who have wearied of life and now carelessly condemn the riches of this world, he offers rebirth and renewal by the simple expedient of holding a pistol in their faces. The shock of imminent death alerts them to the wonders and goodness of life.

When Innocent Smith arrives at Beacon House in a symbolically reanimating high wind, he soon has the once-bored residents dancing, singing, painting, picnicking on the roof, and falling in love. He prevails on them—taking a leaf from Adam Wayne—to establish their own "sovereign state" at Beacon House, one complete with laws, customs, and rituals. After Beacon House and its citizens are brought back to life, a conflict is introduced with the arrival of the usual assortment of enemies determined to stop the spread of Smith's seditious doctrines: Dr. Herbert Warner, the psychologist-criminologist; Dr. Cyrus Pym, a criminological expert from America; and Moses Gould, a "small, resilient Jew." Chesterton's familiar cluster of devils is represented by psychology, sociology, Americanization, science, and the Jews. Wishing to place Innocent Smith in a "lunatic asylum," they are thwarted only because the trial is held at Beacon House according to the laws of the new "state." The combination of Smith's irrepressible Dadaism, the newly won Romanticism of the Beaconians, and their contempt for the rules of evidence overthrow the minions of science and rationalism. Innocent Smith disappears in another wind to take his message to others locked in the ice of custom and reason.

Plainly, this piece of fiction is a lesser one than we have seen so far; and its worst failing is the absolutely bloodless portrait of its characters, including the hero. The characters might come alive if, as in *Notting Hill*, the book had been built on only one plot situation, however fantastic. However, too many

fantasies compete for attention—the redemption of the Beaconians, the walk around the world, the elopements with the wife,
the threats to the pessimists with a pistol, and the trial itself.
In all this "business," the characters, who are feebly conceived
in the first place, seem all the more flaccid; and the didactic
intent becomes more exigent and annoying.

## VI   The Flying Inn

*The Flying Inn* (1914) has more to recommend it as both art
and preachment because Chesterton's wrath is really stirred by
the threats to England of prohibition, Islam, and plutocracy. The
villain of the piece is Lord Ivywood, a wealthy Puritanical
aristocrat who is somehow able to persuade his colleagues in
Parliament to close the inns of England. He finds intellectual
support for his prejudice against alcohol in the doctrine of Islam,
which is being propagandized in England by Ivywood's accom-
plice, Misysra Ammon, a fake prophet from the Middle East.

Opposed to Ivywood and Ammon—and the adoring "blue-
stockings" attracted to an insane cause—are Humphrey Pump,
owner of "The Old Ship" inn,   and Captain Patrick Dalroy, a
romantic Irish adventurer. When they discover the loophole in
Ivywood's new law (that alcohol may be served wherever an
inn sign is posted), they uproot the sign of "The Old Ship,"
load an automobile with barrels of drink, and set out on a cross-
country odyssey to dispense liquor to the suffering natives.

As the two heroes in flight are pursued by the forces of evil,
the book takes something of the shape of *The Ball and the Cross.*
Ivywood has the help not only of the plutocrats but of the
leaders of government (the focus on these corrupt politicians is
symptomatic of Chesterton's state of mind after the Marconi
affair the previous year), all of whom are well-disposed to passing prohibition laws if they do not affect the wealthy.

The other target of *The Flying Ship* is the religion of Islam,
which Chesterton believed was capturing the imagination of
many British intelligentsia in the years before the war. Chesterton condemns not just the prohibitionist element in the Islamic
religion; he strongly suggests that Ivywood is destroying the
concept of the family—has, indeed, begun to gather a harem

on his estate. The very decor of his estate is the repetitious abstract patterning, devoid of any human content, that is indigenous to the Middle East. Islam, for Chesterton, is a serious menace to all the social and religious values of England and the West. Since some Armageddon must occur, the Christians under Dalroy (flying the flag of St. George) meet and defeat the sepoy troops of Ivywood and rescue the heroine from his harem.

## VIII   Tales of the Long Bow

The formula of *The Flying Ship* is repeated in *Tales of the Long Bow* (1925) with almost no change, a sign perhaps of a waning of Chesterton's imagination. This time the battle is between the peasants of England, who wish to continue farming and raising pigs as they have for centuries, and the big business interests, who wish to monopolize the nation's entire pork production. Several faceless, indistinguishable heroes borrow the heraldic sign of the Blue Boar from a nearby inn and begin the struggle against the plutocrats. Calling themselves at first the "Lunatic Asylum," they eventually organize under the tutelary protection of Gurth (Scott's swineherd in *Ivanhoe*, and an example to Carlyle of how the Medieval slave was contented and well-fed, although lacking freedom)

The tide of battle changes when one of the American moguls throws his support to the peasants and helps to arm them as "The League of the Long Bow," descendent from the ancient English yeomanry. The battle lines are drawn, complete with artillery and airplanes; and in the Armageddon that follows the forces of modernism are defeated because of a breakdown in their organization.

The book is one of Chesterton's least successful romance-anatomies; it lacks even the rudiments of characterization and is crushed by the absurdities of the plot. One striking scene, however, is that of the Thames River (or the layer of industrial sludge on its surface) being set afire, while in the background someone recites the Spenserian (or Eliotic) refrain, "Sweet Thames, run softly till I end my song." This scene may also be among the first descriptions in modern fiction of industrial pollution. Another imaginative motif is the career of Horace Hunter, an incompetent bureaucrat whose rise to the inner circles of British government is sporadically charted in the course of the book. His seemingly inevitable, or at least effortless, elevation is a witty comment on the power of the boot-licking technocrat in industrial science. These few triumphant touches are insufficient, however, to sustain the otherwise lifeless and limp work that generally permeates *Tales of the Long Bow.*

## IX   The Return of Don Quixote

*The Return of Don Quixote* (1927), Chesterton's last book-length romance, has a familiar opening situation; both the title and the situation are deceptively artificial and derivative. Again the reader is presented with a small group of rebels against society: the forces of good are dilettantish aristocrats fascinated by things Medieval. Their dabbling in social reform takes a serious turn when they discover the plight of the laborers in the nearby mill town (the situation is a weak imitation of Dickens's *Hard Times*). Organizing for battle under the leadership of a mild-mannered librarian named Herne (who wears a Robin Hood costume), they overthrow the powers of the industrial state and establish a Utopia with Herne as chief executive.

Also familiar to the reader is the material of the subplot, which involves an older man named Hendry, an artisan once famous for the unequalled artist's oils that he manufactured in his private laboratory. Hendry's small business has been destroyed by the ruinous competition with plutocracy, and he himself has been threatened with incarceration in an insane asylum because he refuses to divulge the secrets of his manufacturing process. Hendry is finally saved by the intercession of Murrel, one of Herne's lieutenants, who prevents the old man's falling into the hands of a Dr. Gambrell. This villain is the bureaucrat-scientist who is described as having "the power to invade this house and break up this family and [to] do what he liked with this member of it."

The clear polarities and familiar character-types of the earlier romances emerge as the main materials. However, the typical

conflict of plutocracy versus intelligentsia and peasants is dis-
arranged into a three-cornered struggle because the workers
have no faith in, or love for, the Medieval dreams of Herne's
dilettantes. (Perhaps their lack of faith arises from their not
being a true peasantry but urban slaves.) The Armageddon, in
fact, involves the aristocrats under Herne and the workers
led by the union leader Braintree. The tragic problem of social
injustice shades into irony when, after the laboring classes are
defeated, Braintree is placed on trial for sedition. He is as
contemptuous of the rampant Medievalism of Herne's Utopia
as any plutocrat of *The Napoleon of Notting Hill.*

In such confusion, what can an intelligent man do? Herne's
answer is to relinquish the powers which he had so arduously
won. Chesterton makes clear Herne's realization that his unlimited powers can only lead to corruption and injustice; for a
victory at Armageddon is not a guarantee that the winner will
be humane and wise. The only answer is the restriction of
power; Herne and Murrel go forth as a new Don Quixote and
Sancho Panza to fight the small injustices which occur in any
society. With their departure, Chesterton abandons the neat
political theories and his earlier dream visions of catastrophic
overthrow of the industrial system. Now the emphasis is on the
hopelessness of confrontation in the industrial age, the lack of
communications between men, and the unhealable core of sin
in the human soul.

The end of the book underscores these themes. Herne tempo-
rarily interrupts his life as the knight errant to find his fiancée,
not in a Medieval castle, nor in a seraglio, but in the dark
labyrinths of Limehouse, where she tends the poor and the
sick. A friend describes the rationale for this self-sacrifice:
"There may be people to whom it's senseless to talk about the
flower of chivalry; it sounds like a blossom of butchery. But if
we want the flower of chivalry, we must go right away back to
the root of chivalry. We must go back if we find it in a thorny
place people call theology. We must think differently about
death and free will and loneliness and the last appeal. It's just
the same with the popular things we can turn into fashionable
things; folk dances and pageants and calling everything a
Guild."[23]

Such an answer is both a rebuke to the quasi-Medievalists of the William Morris type, and an implicit modification of Distributism. *The Return of Don Quixote* is the first of Chesterton's romances to offer a specifically Catholic, non-political, non-sociological program for the future. All secular resistance now seems hopeless, with the industrial workers blind to their real needs, and the power of plutocracy apparently invincible. Murrel, trying to discover Hendry's whereabouts at one point in the book, interviews the manager of a department store, who says that he knows nothing about the missing man. Murrel dejectedly says, "I quite recognize that there is nothing you can do. Damn it all, perhaps there is nothing to be done." And nothing *is* done.

Chesterton's departure from the formulas of his early romances makes *The Return of Don Quixote* one of his most thoughtful and provocative fictions. Admittedly, the characters are no more skillfully drawn than are those of his other fictions, but there are numerous fine things that show Chesterton's imaginative powers. One scene, for example, shows Herne voting in a polling booth, but it takes him hours to accomplish this act; as a lover of democracy he had cast his vote, but as an incurable Medievalist he had carefully painted his "X" in gold and in the style of Medieval illuminated letters. Another sequence describing Murrel in the department store has a nightmare intensity paralleled only by Nathaniel West's *Day of the Locust*: "Every now and then they came on the huge shaft or well of a lift; and the congestion was slightly relieved by some people being swallowed up by the earth and others vanishing into the ceiling. Eventually he himself found he was one of those fated, like Aeneas, to descend into the lower world. Here a new and equally interminable pilgrimage began . . ." (102).

## X   Three Plays

Shaw, unmindful of the weaknesses of Chesterton's romances —the didacticism, the weakly developed characters, the fantastic situations—prevailed on his friend (and several others) to take to dramatic writing as a means of increasing his income, but only a few efforts convinced Chesterton that he was not meant to work in this genre. His first play, *Magic* (1913) is a "Fantastic Comedy." Shavian in all its details, it is the best of his plays if only because of the character of the dotty Duke, who indeed may be Chesterton's finest imaginative creation. The playwright gathers the usual puppets at the Duke's country estate where they are to enjoy an evening of entertainment. The cast of characters is comprised of a High Church minister with Christian Socialist leanings; a doctor who is a scientific rationalist; the Duke's niece, a young lady yearning for romance; and her brother from America, a skeptical, "level-headed" businessman. The entertainment is provided by a magician, who stirs in the others various degrees of outrage, skepticism, indifference, or bemused tolerance.

Only the heroine believes in the reality of the magic, which seems to stand for the spiritual realities of life which are so heavily beset by modern business (the young man from America), modern science (the doctor), and the Established Protestant church (the minister). The magician routs them with a silly parlor trick, but he proves himself to be spiritually corrupt because of his association with some invisible "devil spirits" whom he used to torment his opponents. (Again Chesterton has his innings against Spiritualism and black magic.) The play seems intent on proving that there is a supernatural dimension to life which rationalism cannot encompass, but that it must be approached through the mediation of religion. Unfortunately, the thesis is transmitted through some melodramatic gimmickry, a creaky plot, some of the flattest characters Chesterton ever created, and some of the poorest dialogue Chesterton ever wrote.

*The Judgement of Dr. Johnson* (1927), which is no better than *Magic*, may be regarded as Chesterton's major act of obeisance before his literary and philosophical idol. The Dr. Johnson portrayed is Carlylean rather than Boswellian, heroic and pompous, rather than witty and lively. The Shavian influence appears in the main situation: during the American Revolution a young couple, spies from the colonies, establish a salon in London where they entertain the Great Cham, Boswell, John Wilkes, Edmund Burke, and other social lions. The crux of the play hangs on Johnson and Chesterton's thesis that the revolutionary ideas of the times—the feminism, the intellectualism, the democratic frenzy—are somehow organic with a decay in personal morality. The young couples are not only atheists and

142      G. K. CHESTERTON

democrats but also libertines. Dr. Johnson's "judgment" is to
save these young people, when their position is compromised,
and also save their marriage and their morality by freeing them
of their "sham philosophies." In the process, the hero is turned
into an anti-Hanoverian Chestertonian; Chesterton's Johnson is
eager to denigrate wisdom, philosophy, and mere ideas in favor
of the common sense and hard work of ordinary people—"the
nucleus and norm of humanity." The few Boswellian gems allowed to enter the dialogue glimmer momentarily, then disappear in the murk.

The most interesting play *qua* drama that Chesterton wrote
is the unfinished "The Surprise" (1932; published 1952). A Piran-
dellesque exercise, the play has as its hero a playwright who has
been granted his wish to see the characters of his play living
their own lives, "separated from me and my life and living lives
quite different and entirely their own." The characters of his
romantic comedy, having acted his play in the first act, come
alive in the second act (with the magical interference of a
friar, a friend of the playwright), and replay his play as *they*
wish until he screams, "What do you think you are doing with
my play? Drop it! Stop! I am coming down!"

The editor of the published play is certainly correct in pointing out the analogy between God the creator and the human
artist—an analogy which may be observed elsewhere in Chesterton's works. Just as God creates a world and sets man free to do
good or evil, so the artist in the play has created, with divine
help, characters who escape his control. The theological theme
of free will seems less crucial, however, than the artist's shock
and anger at the sudden liberties the actors take with his play.
Does Chesterton perceive a theological dilemma that he prefers
not to handle? Perhaps Chesterton purposefully left the play
unfinished, evading the theological implications of a situation
wherein Man escapes the control of God because of a totally
independent free will.

Whatever the reason for its incomplete state, "The Surprise"
is the most unusual of Chesterton's three dramas, because its
author was forced to come to grips with certain problems of
dramaturgy and seems to have dimly perceived the potential
of pure theater.

## XI   Conclusion

The romances and dramas, whether seriously polemical or merely light entertainments like the Father Brown stories, are continuing skirmishes in the social, political, and intellectual battles that engaged Chesterton in his non-fictional writings. If his novels have lost some of their force, then, it may be because the ideas or problems that originally inspired them are now lost in the wastes of history. It is difficult, for example, in an age of atomic war, to be stirred by an appeal to arm oneself with a longbow; in an age when great nations confront each other with ballistic missiles, it is not amusing to hear of armies fighting in uniforms of Medieval armor and liveries; and, as the British Empire dissolves, one does not wish to be told that salvation lies in English ale and cheese.

Other elements of these fictions are even less germane to the 1970's. Chesterton's obsession with the competition of foreign labor, his fear of an "invasion" of Orientals or Middle Easterners, partakes directly of the Edwardian taste for scare-stories about "invasions" of the British isles.[24] Similarly, his unsavory portraits of Jewish financiers reflect an attitude of anti-Semitism widespread among the ruling classes of prewar Britain. Moreover, Chesterton's characterization and his faith in man's capacity for individual heroism belong similarly to some bygone age. While other novelists developed their special visions of the anti hero, Chesterton transmuted his clerk-heroes and aristocratic dilettantes into Medieval knights.

What is unexpected is that this alteration in character is too often achieved with a magic wand; in a moment these Milquetoasts are suddenly provided with a quantity of wit, strength, personality, cleverness, and the ability to lead. While other novelists of our time have mapped the inner contours of the personality, Chesterton disregards any analysis or dramatization of character. His cocoons metamorphose into butterflies, and the reader must accept the quick change. Ironically, Chesterton, the writer who loved the common man and defended the value of the individual, did not have sufficient patience or love to create warm-blooded fictional characters in his romances.[25]

One excuses Chesterton with the word "romances," for it is

clear that he is a "romancer." He admired Stevenson and the
toy theater. He defended the Victorian melodrama, which has
been recently described as an art form that prizes, above all,
the quality of simplicity—of plot, of theme, and of character.
Nor is it entirely accidental that Chesterton's idol, Dickens, has
been perennially criticized for his "caricatures" and careless
portrayal of characters.

In spite of these flaws (if they are flaws), Chesterton's romances have numerous merits and do not deserve the oblivion
in which they languish at present. Their lively style, their
frequent wittiness of the characters, and especially their imaginative use of symbolic scenes and incidents make them the
equals of other novels that have achieved critical recognition.
For example, Chesterton's imagination is irresistible in such
scenes as "the battle of the lamps," Innocent Smith's walk around
the world, the Orwellian asylum in *The Ball and the Cross*, the
brilliant central situation of *The Man Who Was Thursday*, the
description of Lord Ivywood's estate and harem, and Adam
Wayne's pledge of fealty to Auberon Quin. The didacticism,
the woodenness of the characters, and the frequent lapses of
style should not stand in the way of the re-discovery of these
romances in an era in which nightmare literature, fantasy, absurd
and surrealistic plots, and wildly conceived characters have
become the novelist's stock-in-trade.

## CHAPTER 7

# The Frenzy to Make Something

IN the essay "The Metaphysical Poets" (1921), T. S. Eliot announced that the poet of a bewilderingly complex age must be "more allusive, more indirect, in order to force, to dislocate if necessary language to his meaning."[1] Such poems as *The Waste Land* (1922) and Ezra Pound's *Cantos* (1919 on) were the prototypes of the new poetry—scholarly, obscure, "objective," and allusive. Concealed, if not entirely effaced, was the personality of the poet, which is in line with Eliot's precept that the poet does not have a personality to express but only a medium.[2] The emphasis on "medium" meant that the poet's primary function was to exploit the full range of meanings and effects inherent in individual words. Entirely missing in the new poetry was the security that the reader might gain from hearing a central personality express his emotions or his ideas with a clarity of syntax and directness of diction.

Whether one chooses to see Chesterton as a leader of a nonexistent "Chestertonian school," or, isolated, as a poet injudiciously scratching in the exhausted lodes of Victorian poetry, it is plain that he must be excluded from the poetic revolution of the twentieth century. In seven volumes of poems he shows himself to be all that Eliot and Pound were struggling against—didactic, personal, direct, and expressive. He is, in short, both a counter-Decadent and an antimodernist who goes his own way in poetry as in so many other things. The seven volumes of poems are now available in a one-volume edition, but even so they remain unread, largely because they are unfashionable from whatever perspective one chooses to view them. The truth is that Chesterton perfectly reflects what Eliot diagnosed as "the dissociation of sensibility," that split of emotion and intellect which occurred sometime after the seventeenth century. Chesterton's poetry may be divided into two discrete, partly unsatisfying strains. One type of Chestertonian verse pays homage to the eighteenth century, being rationalistic, satirical, and coldly intellectual; the other belongs to the Romantic tradition of the nineteenth century—more emotional, personal, and rhetorical. While the second variety may have touched the sensibility of the era in which he lived, it is the satiric poetry which (in spite of its dated subject matter) strikes the reader today as more effective.

## I  *The Romantic Verse*

The supreme embodiment of Chesterton's poetry is "The Ballad of the White Horse" (1912), a long, eight-book ballad on the subject of Alfred the Great's fight against the Danes. The thematic keys to the poem are the poet's Christian faith (especially a Mariology evident throughout his works) and his love of old England. The title is derived from the white horses which are carved in the chalk hillsides of England, the mysterious artwork of men living in prehistory and symbolic to Chesterton of English history and culture.

The narrative relates how Alfred regained his courage after near-total defeat; rallied his men (his lieutenants represent the Roman, Celtic, and Saxon roots of England); and, after having a vision of Virgin Mary, defeated the enemy at Ethandune. The turning point is Mary's answer to Alfred's prayer; when she tells him "I tell you naught for your comfort,/ . . . Save that the sky grows darker yet/And the sea rises higher," he is convinced that his cause is pure and selfless and that he can trust himself After the lengthy description of the final campaign against the heathen, the poem ends with the important book entitled "The Scouring of the Horses," in which Alfred is shown as lawgiver and father of his country, as he presides over a small island kingdom which he prefers to the grandeur of a great empire. In his old age, he is called forth to fight the Danes again, for evil will reappear to threaten good men. In the years before the Great War and the Marconi trial, the poet Chesterton has Alfred warn men against a "far century, sad and slow" when the plant growth on the white horse on the hillside will need to be uprooted again; it will be a century filled with "great talk of trend and tide,/ and wisdom and destiny" (the denial of man's free will), and the invaders will not be warriors but men "mild as monkish clerks."

While the poem's didacticism is not so intrusive as it appears in summary, one can admire the poem only as a *tour de force* —as a successful rendering of the traditional ballad narrative. A rare image shines forth ("And hairy men, as huge as sin/ With horned heads, came wading in..."), and even rarer is a profound insight into the human experience:

> There lives one moment for a man
> When the door at his shoulder shakes,
> When the taut rope parts under the pull,
> And the barest branch is beautiful
> One moment, while it breaks.

These briefly discerned treasures do not redeem the long passages of prosaic narration delivered with the incessant beat of the meter. And rarely, as even these quotations show, does the poet exploit the associations and symbolic possibilities of the individual word.

The same criticism may be applied to "Lepanto" (1912), a much-anthologized piece which, John Buchan relates, was chanted by the British soldiers of 1914 to lift their spirits in the trenches.[3] The story of Don John of Austria's victory over the heathen at Lepanto echoes Alfred's situation at Ethandune, but the narrative thrust is blunted by a Swinburnian lushness and a sing-song rhythm which first hypnotizes, then embarrasses:

> Don John pounding from the slaughter-painted poop,
> Purpling all the ocean like a bloody pirate's sloop . . .

And the modern reader finds little to be excited about while reading such lines as "Gun upon gun, ha! ha!/ Gun upon gun, hurrah!/ Don John of Austria/ has loosed the cannonade."

The observable weaknesses of "Lepanto" that take it to the edge of doggerel are evident in much of Chesterton's romantic verse, extending from the early, practically unreadable *The Wild Knight* (1900) through the *Poems* of 1915 (in which "Lepanto" appeared) and *The Ballad of St. Barbara* (1922), to *The Queen of Seven Swords* (1926). Chesterton's problem may be sum-

marized very briefly: whenever he strives for a kind of high
seriousness in his poetry, he is vulnerable to the moribund diction
and overheated phrasing that afflicted so many of the Edwardian
and Georgian poets. One example may suffice—a passage from
"A Wedding in War Time" in the *St. Barbara* volume:

> Our God who made two lovers in a garden,
> And smote them separate and set them free,
> Their four eyes wild for wonder and wrath and pardon
> And their kiss thunder as lips of land and sea:
> Each rapt unendingly beyond the other,
> Two starry worlds of unknown gods at war,
> Wife and not mate, a man and not a brother,
> We thank thee thou hast made us what we are.

There is much that will not bear a second reading: the portentous
tone, the pounding alliteration, the nonsense of some of the
images, and the inanity of the final line. The subject matter
has been stretched beyond the breaking point, and finally sinks
under the weight of the inflated diction. Nowhere in evidence
is Chesterton's typical flash of wit and fresh language.

## II  *The Satirical Verse*

One regrets that Chesterton gave so much of himself to his
"serious" romantic verse, for his real poetic strength was the
satirical verses that place him firmly in that respectable tradition
of English verse that includes the names of Dryden, Pope, Byron,
and Gilbert. (The very mention of these names again suggests
Chesterton's relationship to a "Neoclassical tradition.") In fact,
one may say that satire was Chesterton's forte in both prose and
poetry, beginning with his earliest book, *Greybeards at Play*
(1900), a small volume of satires on such matters as "The One-
ness of the Philosopher with Nature" to the *Poems* of 1932, his
last collection, which includes materials written or published
over a span of years.

Even the *Poems* of 1915, which includes the tremulous religious songs described earlier, contains a number of satirical
poems worthy of note. One which excited much attention when
it first appeared in *Eye-Witness* (May, 1912) is a barb directed

at a Member of Parliament, F. E. Smith (later the Earl of Birkenhead), who had spoken with some agitation against the Welsh Disestablishment Bill, saying that it had "shocked the conscience of every Christian community in Europe." Chesterton not only disliked the Bill, which disendowed the Church of England in Wales as a first step toward Disestablishment (the Church finally was disestablished in Wales in 1920); further, he was annoyed by the impassioned rhetoric of the Parliamentarian. His final stanza neatly skewered the Philistine:

> It would greatly, I must own,
>    Sooth me, Smith!
> If you left this theme alone,
>    Holy Smith!
> For your legal cause or civil
>    You fight well and get your fee;
> For your God or dream or devil
>    You will answer, not to me.
> Talk about the pews and steeples
>    And the cash that goes therewith!
> But the souls of Christian peoples . . .
>    Chuck it, Smith!

The punchy tail-lines, the slangy diction, and the irony make a hard-edged break with the softness of Edwardian poetry.

The acid diction, manipulated with Augustan ease, may be found elsewhere in the 1915 *Poems*. When another member of Parliament, Walter Long, boasted that he was "never standing by while a revolution was going on," Chesterton leaped on the hapless victim with "The Revolutionist," of which a fine triplet is only one of many merits:

> Walter, beware! scorn not the gathering throng,
> It suffers, yet it may not suffer wrong,
> It suffers, yet it cannot suffer Long.

Chesterton also impales some dilettantes who have formed a Shakespeare Memorial League to hold dear the memory of the Bard, by describing them as "Souls most fed with Shakespeare's flame" who "sit unconquered in a ring,/ Remembering him like anything." Also immortalized is the Reverend Isaiah Bunter, a missionary eaten while in cannibal country, who may therefore be said to have "spread religion in a way/ That he did not intend."

As may be deduced from these quotations, Chesterton carries the themes of his prose polemics over into his verse. Cobbett is described in a poem appearing in *The Ballad of St. Barbara* volume as "the horseman of the shires;/ And his face was red with judgment/ And a light of Luddite fires..." The English public gives its warning in an angry poem called "The Secret People":

> There are no folk in the whole world so helpless or so wise.
> There is hunger in our bellies, there is laughter in our eyes;
> You laugh at us and love us, both mugs and eyes are wet:
> Only you do not know us. For we have not spoken yet.

The best poems of the *St. Barbara* volume are the "Songs of Education" that close it. One reveals the lies taught English schoolchildren:

> So that Lancashire merchants whenever they like
> Can water the beer of a man in Klondike,
> Or poison the meat of a man in Bombay;
> And that is the meaning of Empire day.

The *New Poems* of 1932 are almost completely satirical, beginning with the first poem, which deplores an age which "sees Men accumulate and Wealth decay"—and thereby pays homage to Goldsmith and the satiric tradition of the eighteenth century. Many of these poems are delicious fun, as for example "To a Holy Roller," which mocks one of the fulminating Bible-thumpers at the Scopes "monkey-trial":

> "Roll on," said Gilbert to the earth:
> "Roll on," said Byron to the sea:
> Accepting natural features thus,
>      Freely I say, "Roll on" to thee.

In a parody of free verse in *New Poems* (and Chesterton wrote some of the best parodies in the English language), he comments to the sober-sided modern poet that "I can't help wishing you got more fun out of it. . . ." The comment might well serve as a deft criticism of Chesterton's own poetry. When he is serious and somber, wearing the robes of a poet-prophet, his powerful ego splashes about in a mood in which poetic values are easily forgotten. When he looks beyond his self-absorption toward some target, Chesterton can laugh or be scornful as the mood strikes; and his poems take on a vigor and trust that any reader can appreciate.

While it remains true, as Lea says, that Chesterton's poems show an "insensitiveness to the subtler emotional quality of words,"[4] such a quality is expendable in light satiric verse. When he is at his best, Chesterton's verse has some of the prickly quality of the great Augustan satirists; admittedly, such verse blooms on the lower slopes of Parnassus, but it is not without it own excellences. Undoubtedly Chesterton was proudest of the treacly, confessional lyrics warmed over from Swinburne and the Pre-Raphaelites, and the martial moods that he inherited from Kipling and William Ernest Henley. The modern reader, however, is grateful for the large number of high-spirited and light-hearted satiric verses that he wrote so effortlessly and with such gusto.

CHAPTER 8

# Conclusion: The Grip of Reality

SINCE Chesterton's death, it is clear that his works have
suffered through a period of nearly total neglect by both
the academic critics and the more general audience. As this is
written, there is no sign that the neglect is abating. Although
the discontents of the capitalist world are rising (making his
social criticism the most relevant aspect of his thought), his
Distributist program as a whole has little hope of implementa-
tion. His fictions have not been without some influence, to the
political right on such novelists as Charles Williams and C. S.
Lewis, and to the left on such anti-Utopians as Aldous Huxley
and George Orwell. Generally, however, it must be admitted
that these romance-anatomies are unread. Similarly his poems
languish in the limbo staked out (perhaps with justice) for the
minor Edwardian and Georgian versifiers. His Catholic apologetics are now questioned as much by Catholics as by Protestants.[1]

An author may deserve such oblivion, but he deserves it on
the basis of criticism founded on experience and knowledge.
This book has attempted, if only indirectly, to correct a number of misconceptions that currently pass for understanding of
Chesterton. A few myths remain to be exposed, starting with
the widespread belief that Chesterton is best understood as
a Romantic or part of the English Romantic tradition. This
classification has the appearance of being convincing (because
of Chesterton's love of the simple pleasures, his democratic
impulses, his Whitmanlike praise of existence, his rebellious-
ness against society), but it will not withstand close scrutiny.[2]
He is not a "Romantic" by any of those criteria which are frequently used to define that slippery term. If one defines Romanticism as individualism, Chesterton is anti-Romantic, in that he
considers individualism a peculiar modern peril, and advocates

152

in its place the individual's submission, on a secular level, to the power of the family, and on a religious level, to the broad authority of the Church. If Romanticism is defined, as it often is, as an emphasis on feelings, on the emotions, the intuitive powers of man, then Chesterton is far from a Romantic; he always defends the reason as the critical element in man, and preaches that reason must always restrain the emotions and imagination. To the Romantic belief in the goodness of man and the corrupting influence of civilization, Chesterton opposes a different view—a belief in Original Sin and the value of human society.[3] Finally, if the Romantic movement is viewed (as it has been, and very convincingly) as a trend of thought which arrogated to man the powers once ascribed to God, then Chesterton, who always emphasizes the facts of God's creation and God's grace, can hardly be construed as a Romantic.[4]

It is more helpful to categorize Chesterton as a child of the Victorian age, perhaps a late Victorian, combining as he does a number of prejudices and ideas enunciated most clearly by the great Victorians. While rejecting Carlyle's Teutonism, he agreed with him about modern materialism, and felt the same nostalgia for the unity of the Middle Ages. Like Ruskin, he sees the fragmentation of man resulting from industrial society, and turns to the local communities and the restoration of guilds for a remedy. While deploring Arnold's classical rationalism, he is like Arnold in his contempt for Philistine values and in his stress on the necessity of a balance in man's soul. He loves in Dickens the warmth, the joy of life, and the emotional sympathy which enabled the novelist to see into the heart of common humanity. And he is like Newman in his warnings against the powers of the human intellect, and in seeking refuge in the certainties of the Roman Catholic Church. Like all the Victorians he retains a faith in rigid ethical truths, and in the danger to morality created by modern relativism and materialism.[5]

Chesterton may be classified also among those amateur philosophers in English history who tried to create a unified knowledge for their age, men like Sir Francis Bacon, who took all knowledge for his province and planned with his *Instauratio Magna* a synthesis of Renaissance thought, both old and new; or like Herbert Spencer, that other Victorian, who hoped to create

a *Synthetic Philosophy* which would synthesize for his age all of
modern knowledge. Holding that all things are holy, Chesterton
made some pretense of achieving a modern synthesis of man's
experience and knowledge, of pork and pyrotechnics, cakes and
ale, body and spirit. The question which any reader of Chesterton must answer is whether this new synthesis was successful.
Was Chesterton able to hold in perfect suspension, and create a
world view from, the totality of mental, moral, and physical
knowledge, acquired in the twentieth century?

Perhaps not surprisingly, the answer must be in the negative.
Reading through Chesterton's works, one quickly becomes aware
of the vast gaps in Chesterton's experience and thought, either
because of his ignorance or tactical indifference. More than one
critic, for example, has pointed to Chesterton's Puritanical hostility to the subject of man's sexuality. We have seen his unwil-
lingness to readjust his world-view to the implications of an
Einsteinian universe, and one may be rightly suspicious of his
too hasty incuriosity about modern psychology. Typical of Chesterton is his statement in *Heretics* that "Never has there been so
little discussion about the nature of man as now."[6] Yet at the
time he was writing, in 1905, just the opposite was true—there
was nothing being discussed so much as the nature of man.
One remembers with a start the names of the men at the turn
of the century who were redefining the nature of man—Zola,
Bergson, Freud, Proust, and Frazer, to name a few—and is forced
to conclude that Chesterton's ears were shut to the debate.

When Chesterton says "There is one thing needful—everything," one deduces that the catholicity is more rhetorical than
real, disregarding as it does broad areas of man's experience—
the irrational, the modern sense of the absurd, existential *angst*,
sexuality, and even the sense of the tragic. Chesterton had re-
proved the "heretics" for "taking one side of truth and making
it all of truth," but he was himself satisfied with a limited vision
of the truth.[7] Like these others, he could not escape his age,
"a pre-1914 Age of Reason when men believed in the power of
reason and were prepared to use it vigorously and combatively
to prove that they were right and their opponents wrong, [com-
pared to] now, when we are suspicious of any discussion of pure
ideas, and a logic which deals in such clear-cut categories as

'right' or 'wrong' seems pretty crude."[8] The scope of Chesterton's thought was delimited by his Christian humanism, which acted less as a synthesizer than as a magnet which rejects as much material as it selects.

Chesterton was incapable of including in his final synthesis a large number of inescapable facts of modern life. For him, America was a wandering prodigal, Russia almost incomprehensible, Africa non-existent, and Asia a boundless mistake. Philosophies and religions of alien lands (or of an exotic nature) were rejected on the assumption that they contained nothing useful for the Western mind; into the trash-can went Islam, pantheism, atheistic rationalism, Christian science, Eastern mysticism, and all forms of Protestantism. Acting as the Colonel Blimp of the English middle-brow audience, he ignored the impressions of the Impressionists, abominated the fragmented art of the cubists, and seemed oblivious to the revolution occurring in poetry and the novel. Although well-read, possessed of a prodigious memory, and undeniably gifted, Chesterton always draws on a fairly narrow band of intellectual and emotional responses to the complex issues of his times.

One may compare him with the grand figure of Dr. Johnson, who also fought a rear-guard action against an advancing enemy. Chesterton said of Johnson that he combined "a great external carelessness with considerable internal care." This insight provides a final clue for an understanding of Chesterton. On the outside one sees Chesterton cheering and waving his arms, extolling the wonders of ale, postboxes, English roads, bacon, detective stories, and rustic dancing. Life is a great orange to be squeezed of its juices. One does not feel, however, while reading him, that there is that complete loss of self, that abandonment of mind recommended by D. H. Lawrence and evident in the writings of, say, Walt Whitman or Thomas Wolfe. The enthusiasm is never permitted to erase or diffuse the personality, but is always under the command of a powerful English commonsense. Father Kelly has rightly said of Chesterton, "Mystic, traditionalist, optimist, medievalist, democrat, these he was, but never at the expense of reason and intelligence."[9] Faced with the complexity, the absurdity of the universe, Kierkegaard preached the need for a "leap" to faith, which met Ignatius

Loyola's requirement of "The sacrifice of the intellect." One may say that Chesterton never sacrificed his intellect; faced with the abyss of universal absurdity and irrationality, he always made his "leap" to reason and the sanctuary of a coherent world-view.

The decline of Chesterton's reputation in our time may be attributed to the aversion the modern mind feels for such rationalistic Thomism. Because the modern mind is generally not Thomist, Catholic, rationalistic, or Distributist, the modern critic irrationally deprecates or ignores Chesterton the artist. This proscription is itself irrational because great artists do not survive by virtue of their ideas or philosophy; the ideas of Shakespeare, or Milton, or Sophocles were the commonplaces of their times, and they remain commonplaces when extracted from their artistic context. It has become axiomatic in modern criticism that great literature continues to shape our thought and sensibility less by the philosophical content than by the skill with which it is expressed, i.e., by the author's imaginative use of language.

If Chesterton is ever to be revived, it must be on the basis of a rhetorical skill that occasionally reaches the level of high poetry. Chesterton would reject this thesis as "art for art's sake," and take it as a final measure of his failure as propagandist and teacher. Nevertheless it has delivered many a lesser writer and thinker from the ravages of time and oblivion.

It must be admitted from the start that Chesterton has been defended along rhetorical lines almost continuously since his death, but the defense has concentrated almost entirely on the element of paradox in his work. As a man sensitive to the numerous contradictions of human experience, this "man of paradoxes" forged a style which reflected those contradictions. This has been taken as proof that he was more "poetic" and had a profounder view of life than is ordinarily assumed. Thus Hugh Kenner (who has written a book on *Paradox in Chesterton*) writes that paradox was for Chesterton "a key to new awareness" and a "means to truth and a means to art."[10]

That paradox was the key to his art and thought was certainly not a conscious assumption on Chesterton's part. He rarely mentions it, and never with pride; in one essay he says that it has "very painful memories for me."[11] Chesterton is undoubtedly alluding to the frequent criticism that any author might write paradoxes all day if he wished—a palpable hit, as anyone may discover by experiment. The cheap effect achieved by the paradox has won Chesterton an audience, but also may have repelled other potential readers.

A more trenchant criticism of the paradoxical style is that it does not testify to the writer's catholicity or profundity. Paradoxes have content as well as form, direction as well as shape. One might write thousands of paradoxes which would offend Chesterton (as did Oscar Wilde, in fact), such as: "An excessive love of the family will tear it apart," "The most catholic religion is the religion of self," and "Seen icons are good, but unseen ones are better." These all satisfy the form of the paradox but do not follow the central thrust of Chesterton's philosophy. The final test of the paradox is that it contains no ambiguity: one may be shocked by it, but one always knows what it means and can soon enough discover its intellectual premises. Paradox in Chesterton is another stratagem used to control the imagination, to restrain the mind; it is more evidence of that "leap to reason" so characteristic of Chesterton. Because Chesterton's paradoxes continually pull the reader toward the central world-view—with which he may dissent—they are hardly a solid basis on which to erect a defense of Chesterton.

The feature of Chesterton's style which has so far been insufficiently appreciated is a concreteness, or particularism, that is always a sign of a dynamic imagination. It is this quality that explains Chesterton's unceasingly energetic writing. The philosophy itself—Catholic with some touches of Puritanism, rationalistic, highly ethical, stressing personal responsibility and self-reliance—would be a chilly thing, especially in combination with a totally paradoxical style. Yet Chesterton's admirers know what the world may yet discover: that each essay is fresh, original, and imaginative because of the author's ability to explain the most abstruse matters with examples, analogies, and illustrations from various levels of experience. The philosophy may be centripetal, but the vision is centrifugal; the result is a balance or tension unique since the prose writers of the seventeenth century.

This concreteness—what he called "my lifelong belief in particularism"—of course has its analogies in the Thomistic thought

to which he was dedicated. "True religion," he says in *Avowals
and Denials*, "tries to express truths as facts, and make abstract
things as plain and solid as concrete things."[12] The sentence is
interesting in that it suggests something of Chesterton's desire
to be both teacher and poet. Belloc speaks for many of Chesterton's readers when he says that he is "astonished" at Chesterton's
"ability in illustration."[13] To the service of his religion and
thought, Chesterton calls all the devices of the poet—examples,
descriptions, specific details, *exempla*, similes, metaphors, and
analogies, as well as paradoxes, some drawn from everyday
experience, and some from his reading.

Occasionally his imagination receives its momentum from
some concrete object or experience and works centrifugally to
relate that innocuous item to his world-view; thus his essays on
such topics as cheese, lamp-posts, aids to golf, eyebrows, nudists,
turnpikes, taffy, skeletons, ugly things, the pillory, telegraph
poles, and a piece of chalk. This type of essay perfectly illustrates his belief that "almost any subject, considered as a subject,
contains stuff and substance enough for an essay, when we consider that its origin and object, and material and design, and
relation to other things, are all subjects in themselves."[14] In other
essays, the movement of the mind is at least partly tangential,
showing the subject's "relation to other things" before spiralling
inward. The mind ranges up and down the scale of experience,
always searching for the vivid illustration, connecting by means
of similes and analogies, and clarifying abstract issues with
*exempla*. Thus the essay on Tennyson in *The Uses of Diversity*
touches on modern science, the Huns, ontogeny recapitulating
phylogeny, the French Revolution, Byron, and man as Yahoo.

While the reader has already observed the sprightliness of
Chesterton's imagination, diction, and style, a few more par-
ticulars may clarify these generalizations. Frequently the reader
is given simple similes: "The good mystery story should narrow
its circles like an eagle about to swoop."[15] Simple metaphors:
"I saw . . . that the modern world is an immense and tumultuous
ocean, full of monstrous and living things . . . [and] across the
top of it is spread thin, a very thin sheet of ice, of wicked wealth
and of lying journalism."[16] Complex metaphor: Gothic architecture "is, first, . . . alive, and, second, . . . on the march. It is the

Church Militant; it is the only fighting architecture. All its spires are spears at rest; and all its stones are stones asleep in a catapult. In that instant of illusion, I could hear the arches clash like swords as they crossed each other."[17] Analogy (often for purposes of *reductio ad absurdum*): "How could physical science prove that man is not depraved? You do not cut a man open to find his sins. You do not boil him until he gives forth the unmistakable green fumes of depravity. How could physical science find any traces of a moral fall? What traces did the writer to expect to find? Did he expect to find a fossil Eve with a fossil apple inside her? Did he suppose that the ages would have spared for him a complete skeleton of Adam attached to a slightly faded fig-leaf?"[18]

One is tempted to continue with quotations, but readers of Chesterton are aware that such gems may be found throughout his articles. One must marvel at the imagination which can create a kind of metaphoric fusion out of the rush of images. Aside from being the perfect correlative of Chesterton's Thomism, the effect of this density of images is something close to poetry. Perhaps this is what Michael Mason means when he says that Chesterton, by "embracing the vulgar," has provided one solution to that "dissociation of sensibility" that Eliot diagnosed as a serious flaw in modern literature.[19] The only thing lacking to make this kind of poetry "metaphysical" is a degree of sophistication characteristic of only the greatest geniuses.

One is forced to conclude that Chesterton is most poetic when he least thinks about it—when he is writing those ephemeral pieces of journalism under the pressure of deadline. In the "serious" poems and romances, his creative imagination is stifled by the abstract idea. In the essays, although the world-view continues to act as underpinning, the images flow freely, the mind grasps and puts to use the diversity of life. The effect on the reader is a high order of pleasure that comes from wit, unusual juxtapositions and parallels, and the heterogeneity of life. In this richness of vision, even though it lacks sophistication, one may discern a hope for a return to Chesterton.

# Notes and References

Because Chesterton's essays appeared in periodicals long before they were collected, the footnotes, where necessary, cite the title of the article as well as the collection in which it appears. After the initial citation to a book, subsequent citations appear in parentheses in the text, and refer to the same edition.

## Preface

1. Hugh Kenner, *Paradox in Chesterton* (New York, 1947), p. 11.
2. *Leo Tolstoy*, with Edward Garnett (London, 1904), p. 4.
3. Cecil Chesterton is the only critic to argue that his brother's views changed radically, no doubt because of the early perspective; his *G. K. Chesterton: a Criticism* (1908) sees the early skepticism and Socialism writ large. Chesterton himself admitted to "not altering my opinions quickly enough" (*Autobiography*, p. 251). The only sense in which he believed that he changed was in his having become "more militant and in a sense more simple" (Introduction to *Come to Think of It*). His biographer, Maisie Ward, concludes that "Chesterton himself changed less than almost anyone I have ever known or studied, and he would have claimed that the possession of fundamental principles made possible an unusually detached view of the changing scenes of human life and opinion." *Return to Chesterton* (London, 1952), p. 6.

## Chapter One

1. Chesterton had already had at least two poems published in the commercial media. See Sullivan, *Bibliography*, pp. 123, 151.
2. The terms appear everywhere in his works, but see especially "The Futurists," *Avowals and Denials*, pp. 119–27; "Gilbert and Sullivan," *The Eighteen Eighties* (Cambridge, 1930), p. 136; on modern art, "The Mystagogue," *A Miscellany of Men* (London, 1926); "Oscar Wilde" and "Ibsen" in *A Handful of Authors* (London, 1953); on the modern novel, "On Philosophy versus Fiction," *All is Grist* (New York, 1932); on Joyce, "On Phases of Eccentricity," *All I Survey* (London, 1933).
3. Maisie Ward, *Gilbert Keith Chesterton*, p. 25.

4. *Ibid.*, p. 30.

5. "Elizabeth Barrett Browning," *The Common Man* (London, 1950), p. 186.

6. "On the Comic Spirit," *Generally Speaking* (London, 1937), p. 176.

7. *Appreciations and Criticisms of the Works of Charles Dickens* (London, 1911), p. 170.

8. "On Philosophy versus Fiction," *All is Grist*, p. 99.

9. "On Reading," *The Common Man*, p. 22.

10. *Robert Louis Stevenson* (New York, 1928), p. 18. See also Chesterton's statement that "You will begin to know what is all that any art critic needs to know; what the artist is driving at; and why he drove in this direction and not in that." *The Resurrection of Rome* (London, 1930), p. 86.

11. For example, Suzanne Langer says ". . . every critic worth his salt has enough literary intuition to know that *the way of saying things* is somehow all-important." (Italics in original.) *Feeling and Form* (New York, 1953), p. 208.

12. Cecil Chesterton, *Gilbert K. Chesterton: a Criticism*, p. 75.

13. "On Mr. Epstein," *Come to Think of It* (London, 1930), p. 73.

14. *Ibid.*

15. *The End of the Armistice* (New York, 1940), pp. 195–96.

16. "On Algernon Charles Swinburne," *All is Grist*, pp. 251–52.

17. Cecil Chesterton, *Gilbert K. Chesterton*, p. 79.

18. "The Pantomime," *The Common Man*, p. 57.

19. *Robert Browning* (London, 1964), p. 114.

20. Northrop Frye, "Towards Defining an Age of Sensibility," *English Literary History* (June, 1956), pp. 144–52. Reprinted in *Eighteenth-Century English Literature*, ed. James Clifford (New York: Oxford U. Press, 1959), pp. 311–18.

21. The critic is George H. Ford in *Dickens and His Readers* (New York: W. W. Norton and Co., 1965), 240–43.

22. *Charles Dickens* (New York, 1965), p. 290.

23. Related in Cyril Clemens, *Chesterton as Seen by his Contemporaries* (Webster Groves, Mo., 1939,) p. 131.

24. E. M. Forster, *Aspects of the Novel* (New York: Harcourt, Brace and World, 1954), pp. 78–79.

25. G. K. Chesterton, *Appreciations and Criticisms of the Works of Charles Dickens*, p. 15.

26. *Heretics* (London, 1960), p. 290.

27. *Autobiography* (1936), p. 229.

28. William Irvine, *The Universe of G.B.S.*, p. 339. Irvine concurs, calling it "the soundest and most brilliant contribution" to the criticism

of Shaw. St. John Ervine, another biographer of Shaw, says Chesterton's work "is the best book on Shaw that has been written and will probably be the best that will ever be written." *Bernard Shaw: His Life, Work and Friends* (New York, 1956), p. viii.

29. *George Bernard Shaw* (New York, 1956), p. 186.

30. *G. F. Watts* (London, 1904), p. 115.

31. Holbrook Jackson, *The Eighteen-Nineties*, p. 269.

32. *Robert Louis Stevenson*, p. 107.

33. *Chaucer* (London, 1958), p. 9.

34. On the Queen's death, see "Queen Victoria" in *Varied Types* (New York, 1909); on "The Great Gusto" see "On the Prison of Jazz," *Avowals and Denials*, p. 96; on Victorian virtues, see "Three Foes of the Family," *The Well and the Shallows* (New York, 1935); on the verities, see *The End of the Armistice*, p. 183. See also "A Neglected Originality," *Lunacy and Letters* (New York, 1958), pp. 50–55.

35. "On the Way of the World," *All is Grist*, pp. 71–72.

36. See the essays "A Grammar of Shelley" and "Browning and his Ideal" in *A Handful of Authors*.

37. *G. F. Watts*, pp. 87–88 and 91.

38. "On Maltreating Words," *Generally Speaking*, p. 163.

39. "Hamlet and the Psycho-Analyst," *Fancies versus Fads* (New York, 1923), pp. 25–26.

40. "The Sultan," *A Miscellany of Men*, p. 202.

41. The distinction between "sign" and "symbol" is developed fully in Suzanne Langer's *Philosophy in a New Key* (New York, 1951). Note especially: "A concept is all that a symbol really conveys. But just as quickly as the concept is symbolized to us, our own imagination dresses it up in a private, personal *conception*, which we can distinguish from the communicable public concept only by a process of abstraction" (p. 70).

42. On St. Paul's see "An Essay on Two Cities," *All Things Considered* (New York, 1956), p. 53; on the Trade Unionist's badge, see "The Poetry of the Revolution," *Utopia of Usurers* (New York, 1917), p. 212; see also, in *The Resurrection of Rome*, the Church's use of graven images, which "stand for this strange mania of Certitude . . . that something is really true; true in every aspect and from every angle" (p. 90).

43. "Introduction" to John Ruskin, *Poems* (London: George Routledge, 1908), p. vi.

44. "On Blake and his Critics," *Avowals and Denials*, p. 130.

45. "The Middleman in Poetry," *Sidelights on New London and Newer York* (London, 1932), p. 210.

46. *William Blake,* p. 130.

47. "Detective Novels," *Generally Speaking,* p. 2.

48. "The Taste for Milton," *A Handful of Authors,* p. 76; see also his statement in "On Literary Cliques" that "The ideal condition is that the poet should put his meaning more and more into the language of the people, and that the people should enjoy more and more of the meaning of the poet." *Avowals and Denials,* p. 111.

49. M. Versfeld, "Chesterton and St. Thomas," *English Studies in Africa,* IV, 1 (March, 1961), 132.

50. *The Resurrection of Rome,* p. 317.

51. See the "Introduction" to Ruskin's *Poems* which argues that "Those who talk of the artist's nature swelling and expanding, those who talk of outbreak, licence and overflowing of art are people with no sort of feeling of what art is. Art means diminution. If what you want is largeness, the universe as it is is large enough for anybody" (p. vii). For another view, see Norman Brown, *Love's Body* (New York, 1966).

52. "An Essay on Two Cities," *All Things Considered,* p. 53.

53. *Tales of the Long Bow* (New York, 1925), p. 108.

## Chapter Two

1. Malcolm Muggeridge, "G.K.C.," *New Statesman* (August 23, 1963), p. 226.

2. "On Bigness and America," *Come to Think of It,* p. 224. On being a Medievalist, see "On Architecture," *Generally Speaking,* p. 251.

3. Jeffrey Hart argues for the political interest, "In Praise of Chesterton," *Yale Review,* LIII (May, 1964), p. 57; Belloc argues for a religious center, *On the Place of Gilbert Chesterton in English Letters* (London, 1940), *passim.*

4. "Reflections on a Rotten Apple," p. 227.

5. "The Last Turn," *The Well and the Shallows,* pp. 131–32.

6. "The Man on Top," *A Miscellany of Men,* p. 219.

7. On ugliness, "The Aristocratic 'Arry," *A Miscellany of Men,* p. 174; on women, "Three Foes of the Family," *The Well and the Shallows,* p. 148; on the quality of life, "Pageants and Dress," *The Uses of Diversity,* p. 130.

8. "The Universal Stick," *What's Wrong With the World* (London, 1912), p. 123.

9. "The War on Holidays," *Utopia of Usurers,* p. 28.

10. "On Dialect and Decency," *Avowals and Denials,* p. 72.

11. "The Ascetic at Large," *The Well and the Shallows,* p. 122.

12. *The Common Man,* p. 1.

13. On the asylum and rapids, "The Humour of H. M. Bateman," *G.K.C. as M.C.* (London, 1929), p. 138; on the Walpurgisnacht, see "On the Prison of Jazz," *Avowals and Denials*, p. 91.

14. "The Mad Official," *A Miscellany of Men*, p. 49.

15. *The Outline of Sanity* (London, 1926), p. 50.

16. "The Legal Lady," *Fancies versus Fads*, pp. 60–61.

17. "Liberalism: a Sample," *Utopia of Usurers*, p. 112.

18. "The Empire of the Ignorant," *Utopia of Usurers*, p. 159.

19. "How Mad Laws are Made," *Fancies versus Fads*, p. 183.

20. "I Say a Democracy Means . . . ," privately printed, New York, 1941. See also *The Nation*, January 26, 1911.

21. "The Chartered Libertine," p. 248.

22. "The Mad Official," *A Miscellany of Men*, pp. 49–51.

23. "On Political Secrecy," pp. 92–93.

24. "The Miser and his Friends," *A Miscellany of Men*, pp. 141–42.

25. "Limericks and Counsels of Perfection," *All Things Considered*, p. 115.

26. Cecil Chesterton defined "Progressive Evolution" as a "religion"; see *Gilbert K. Chesterton*, p. 102.

27. "The Evolution of Slaves," *Fancies versus Fads*, p. 212.

28. "A Working-Man's History of England," *Utopia of Usurers*, p. 88.

29. *A Short History of England* (New York, 1917), p. 193.

30. On Mary Queen of Scots, see *Revaluations: Studies in Biography* (London, 1931); also "If Don John of Austria had Married Mary Queen of Scots," in *If, or History Rewritten* (New York, 1931); on the battle of Hattin, see *The New Jerusalem* (New York, 1921), p. 259; on the coming of the Hanovers, see the *Short History*, and the essays "Who Killed John Keats?" and "On the Closed Conspiracy," in *Come to Think of It*.

31. "Who Killed John Keats?" *Come to Think of It*, pp. 82–83.

32. "Milton and Merry England," *Fancies versus Fads*, pp. 264–66. Cecil calls his brother "a Tory of the seventeenth or early eighteenth century, born out of his due time. In the Cabinet of Bolingbroke, he would have found quite a sympathetic atmosphere." *Gilbert K. Chesterton*, p. 195. Chesterton said "my own sympathies [are] sometimes with the revolutionary and sometimes with the reactionary." "On the Staleness of Revolt," *All I Survey*, p. 44. See also "On Jonathan Swift," *All I Survey*, pp. 82–87.

33. "Milton and Merry England," *Fancies versus Fads*, p. 266. For a melancholy look at the pre-industrial world, see Peter Laslett, *The World We Have Lost* (New York, 1965), pp. 28–52.

34. *William Cobbett* (New York, 1926), p. 5.

35. "The Mad Official," *A Miscellany of Men*, p. 49.

36. *What I Saw in America* (New York, 1922), p. 126.

37. See for example *Irish Impressions* (New York, 1920), pp. 206–11, and *Eugenics and Other Evils* (London, 1922), pp. 1–2.

38. See his early warnings against the rebirth of German militarism in the pamphlet "How to Help Annexation" (London, 1918), and see also "On Suicide: North and South," *All I Survey*, pp. 174–79.

39. "Utopias," *G.K.C. as M.C.*

40. See "Wine when It Is Red," in *All Things Considered* and "Fear of the Film" in *Fancies versus Fads*. For the French background of the anti-Semitism see John R. Harrison, *The Reactionaries* (New York, 1967), pp. 28–30.

41. "The Aristocratic 'Arry," *A Miscellany of Men*, p. 178.

42. *The New Jerusalem*, p. 272.

43. "William Cobbett," *G.K.C. as M.C.*, p. 107.

44. "Dickens as Santa Claus," *G.K.C. as M.C.*, p. 92.

45. "The Nameless Man," *A Miscellany of Men*, p. 29.

46. "On Peasant Proprietorship," p. 292.

47. "The Tower of Babel," *Utopia of Usurers*, p. 175. Chesterton fought to the end; in the last months of his life, he wrote to Maurice Reckitt that the "mortal danger, to me, is the rehabilitation of Capitalism. . . . This is the mountainous peril that towers in my mind." Reckitt, *The World and the Faith*, p. 59.

### Chapter Three

1. "The Man in the Field," p. 58.

2. Chesterton called it a "pretty bad book." Clemens, *Chesterton as seen by his Contemporaries*, p. 134.

3. *The Resurrection of Rome* (London, 1930), p. 245.

4. "On the Fossil of a Fanatic," *Avowals and Denials*, p. 127.

5. "On the One-Party System," *Avowals and Denials*, p. 150.

6. "Why Protestants Prohibit," *The Well and the Shallows*, pp. 262–63.

7. Reckitt, *The World and the Faith*, p. 76.

8. "The Crime of the Communist," *The Scandal of Father Brown*, in *The Father Brown Omnibus* (New York, 1933), p. 930.

9. "The Poetry of the Revolution," *Utopia of Usurers*, p. 213.

10. *The End of the Armistice*, p. 95. In *The Well and the Shallows*, he calls Communism "the only complete and logical working model of Capitalism." See "Sex and Property," pp. 234–35.

11. See "On the Atheist Museum," *Avowals and Denials*, pp. 27–29; see also "The Sun Worshipper," *A Miscellany of Men*, pp. 60–61.

12. "Beginning of the Quarrel," *Outline of Sanity*, p. 6.

13. P. 170.

14. "The Homelessness of Jones," *What's Wrong With the World*, p. 76.

15. "On Mr. Thomas Gray," *All I Survey*, p. 151.

16. "On Education," *All I Survey*, pp. 192–93 and 196.

17. *The Outline of Sanity*, p. 128.

18. "More Thoughts on Christmas," *The Uses of Diversity*, p. 146.

19. "Apologia," *G.K.C. as M.C.*, p. 267. Speaking of Leo XIII's Encyclical on Labour, Chesterton said, "he was saying then exactly what we are saying now. 'As many as possible of the working classes should become owners.' " *The Catholic Church and Conversion*, pp. 99–100.

20. *The Outline of Sanity*, pp. 180–81.

21. "On the Return to the Land," *Avowals and Denials*, p. 66.

22. *The Outline of Sanity*, p. 172.

23. "Do We Agree?" (Hartford, Conn., 1928), p. 48.

24. "On the Bad Word for Guild," *All is Grist*, pp. 226–28.

25. *The Return of Don Quixote* (New York, 1927), p. 265.

26. *The Crimes of England*, pp. 107–8.

27. *The End of the Armistice*, p. 72.

28. "Erin Go Bragh," *G.K.C. as M.C.*, pp. 110–11.

29. *The Crimes of England*, pp. 107–8.

30. "The Empire of the Insect," *What's Wrong With the World*, p. 265.

31. "The Sentimentalism of Divorce," *Fancies versus Fads*, p. 149. Two good discussions of the family as a political unit are in "Turning Inside Out" and "A Defence of Dramatic Unities," both in *Fancies versus Fads*.

32. "The Drift from Domesticity," pp. 43–44. See also "On the Instability of the State," *Avowals and Denials*, p. 138.

33. "The Yule Log and the Democrat," *The Uses of Diversity*, pp. 139–40.

34. On "refusing to make a chair" see "Science and the Eugenists," *Utopia of Usurers*, pp. 39–40; on "indulging a whim," see "The Wildness of Domesticity," *What's Wrong With the World*, p. 57.

35. "The Enemies of Property," *What's Wrong With the World*, p. 47.

36. *The Superstition of Divorce* (London, 1920), pp. 30–31.

37. *Eugenics and Other Evils* (London, 1922), p. 10.

38. Wells, "About Chesterton and Belloc," *The New Age* (January 11, 1908), pp. 209–10; reprinted in *An Englishman Looks at the World* (London, 1914); West, *G. K. Chesterton* (London, 1915).

*Chapter Four*

1. On modern thought, see "On the New Insularity," *All is Grist,* p. 83; on the need for philosophy, see "The Revival of Philosophy— Why?" *The Common Man,* p. 173.

2. "Why I am a Catholic," *The Thing,* p. 76.

3. For brief exegeses of St. Thomas Aquinas's thought, see Gordon Leff, *Medieval Thought* (Baltimore, 1958), pp. 211–24, and Frederick Copleston, S. J., *A History of Philosophy,* II (New York, 1962), pp. 21–155.

4. The letter to Pope, September 29, 1725, is frequently reprinted; see Alan McKillop, *English Literature from Dryden to Burns* (New York, 1948), pp. 140–41.

5. Karl Phleger, *Wrestlers with Christ* (London, 1936), p. 170. Etienne Gilson called it "the best piece of apologetic the century had produced," adding that all the works after it were "a variation on the same theme." Clemens, *Chesterton as Seen by his Contemporaries,* pp. 149–50.

6. *Orthodoxy* (London, 1957), pp. 1–2.

7. "Frozen Free Thought," *The Well and the Shallows,* p. 208; on the "anti-intellectual impasse" of Lawrence, see "The End of the Moderns," *The Common Man,* p. 201; on the "fury of sex," see "Rabelaisian Regrets," *The Common Man,* p. 125.

8. "On Twilight Sleep," *Come to Think of It,* p. 161.

9. The "balance of the mind" is described in "On New Capitals," *Generally Speaking;* "the central point of sanity" in "The Pagoda of Progress," *Fancies versus Fads.*

10. "The Revival of Philosophy—Why?" *The Common Man,* p. 174.

11. "On Shaw and His Black Girl," *Avowals and Denials,* p. 20.

12. "The Return to Religion," p. 79.

13. "On the Atheist Museum," *Avowals and Denials,* p. 26.

14. "On the Real Animal," *Avowals and Denials,* p. 84.

15. Clemens, *Chesterton as Seen by His Contemporaries,* p. 9.

16. "The Sceptic as Critic," *The Thing,* pp. 13–14. For other discussions of ends and means, see "Logic and Lawn Tennis," *The Thing;* "On Aids to Golf," *Generally Speaking;* "The False Photographer" and "The Sultan," *A Miscellany of Men;* "On a Censorship for Literature," and "On the New Poetry" in *Come to Think of It.*

17. "The Futurist," *Uses of Diversity,* p. 80. See also *Orthodoxy,* p. 48. For the modern Protestants, see "On the Truth of Legends," *All is Grist,* p. 186.

18. "On Business Education," *All is Grist,* p. 22.

19. "On the Truth of Legends," *All is Grist,* p. 187.

20. "Authority the Unavoidable," *What's Wrong with the World*, p. 204.

21. *The Resurrection of Rome*, p. 305.

22. "On the Romance of Childhood," *All is Grist*, p. 155.

23. On dreams of Empire, see *The Resurrection of Rome*, pp. 303–8; on Tolstoy's humanism, see "Tolstoy," *Varied Types*, p. 142.

24. On local patriotism, see "The Enchanted Man," and "The Wrong Incendiary," both in *A Miscellany of Men*; "My Name Village," *G.K.C. as M.C.*

25. Clemens, *Chesterton as seen by his Contemporaries*, p. 42. Frances too had a love of "local products, little shops, small industries, everything of the neighborhood." Ada Chesterton, *The Chestertons* (London, 1941), p. 78. On similar principles Chesterton wanted radios refused "those who would really be much better without them." "On Broadcasting," *Generally Speaking*, p. 32.

26. "Boswell," *G.K.C. as M.C.*, p. 3.

27. "Gates and Gate-Crashers," *Sidelights*, p. 53; *The Outline of Sanity*, p. 193.

28. "Literary London," *G.K.C. as M.C.*, p. 32. See also *The Resurrection of Rome*, pp. 14, 126.

29. "On the Movies," *Generally Speaking*, p. 63.

30. "The Empire of the Insect," *What's Wrong With the World*, p. 259.

31. On Pantheism, *Orthodoxy*, pp. 122–23; also, "Concerning a Strange City," *The Common Man*, p. 220. On Oriental Pantheism and "Cosmic Unity," see "The Separatist and Sacred Things," *A Miscellany of Men*, p. 165. He says in another essay in this latter book that the Devil has always been frightening because of his "shapelessness." "The Mystagogue," p. 146. See especially *Orthodoxy*, pp. 161–62.

32. *Orthodoxy*, p. 134.

33. *The New Jerusalem*, p. 262.

34. "On Flags," *Generally Speaking*, p. 89.

35. "On the Classics," *Come to Think of It*, pp. 56–57.

36. "The Superstition of School," *The Common Man*, p. 39.

37. *Orthodoxy*, p. 25.

38. *The Outline of Sanity*, p. 204.

39. *The Resurrection of Rome*, p. 83.

40. *Sartor Resartus*, ch. vii.

41. "Is Darwin Dead?" *Fancies versus Fads*, p. 222.

42. "Strikes and the Spirit of Wonder," *Fancies versus Fads*, p. 240.

43. "On Sophistication," *All is Grist*, p. 233.

44. *Summa Theologica*, Part I, question 39, article 8. See also

William F. Lynch, S.J., *Christ and Apollo* (New York, 1963), for a rehandling of the same problems.

45. Margaret Clarke, "Chesterton the Classicist," *Dublin Review*, CCXXIV (First quarter, 1955), pp. 51–67.

## Chapter Five

1. P. 170. Chesterton's general attitude toward the Orient is expressed in the sentence, "I do not know the East; nor do I like what I know." "The School for Hypocrites," *What's Wrong With the World*, p. 235. His antipathy for Oriental philosophy and religion is documented in "On Europe and Asia," *Generally Speaking*; "On the Simplicity of Asia," *All I Survey*; "The Separatist and Sacred Things," *A Miscellany of Men*; and "The Japanese," *The Uses of Diversity*.

2. "The Mistake of the Machine," *The Wisdom of Father Brown*, in *The Father Brown Omnibus*, p. 307. For more on free will, see "The Return to Religion," *The Well and the Shallows*; "On the Science of Sociology," *Avowals and Denials*.

3. *The Everlasting Man* (New York, 1955), pp. 33, 44.

4. Ward, *Gilbert Keith Chesterton*, p. 620, quoting Clemens, *Chesterton as Seen by his Contemporaries*, pp. 150–51.

5. *St. Thomas Aquinas* (New York, 1956), p. 148.

6. *Ibid.*, p. 42. Taken strictly, the definition suggests Immanence, but Chesterton almost certainly did not mean this; the remainder of his discussion centers on "the body of Christ," and God, "when he worked in the workshop of Joseph." Chesterton's vagueness on this point will continue to bother the critics. F. A. Lea rightly says that Chesterton was "very weak on pantheism." *The Wild Knight of Battersea* (New York, 1947), p. 23. Aodh de Blacam argues that the historicity of the Incarnation is central to Chesterton's thought, which is true enough; to call it, as de Blacam does, "a sort of mystical materialism" is to run counter to Chesterton's belief in God's transcendence. "Defender of the Faith: Chesterton's First Conversion," *The Irish Monthly* (January, 1945), pp. 47–55.

7. Patrick Braybrooke, *I Remember G. K. Chesterton*, p. 67.

8. *The Catholic Church and Conversion* (New York, 1961), p. 60.

9. *Christendom in Dublin* (London, 1933), pp. 77–78; similarly *The Catholic Church and Conversion*, pp. 85–86.

10. *The Catholic Church and Conversion*, p. 83.

11. "A Spiritualist Looks Back," *The Thing* (London, 1929), p. 179.

12. "On Psycho-Analysis," *Come to Think of It*, p. 61.

13. *Irish Impressions*, p. 217.

14. *William Cobbett*, p. 38.

15. "Is Humanism a Religion?" *The Thing*, p. 34. On witchcraft, he says, "I am absolutely certain that there is such a thing as Witchcraft. I impute a belief in it to common sense, to experience and the records of experience, and to a broad view of humanity as a whole." "The Dangers of Necromancy," *The Common Man*, p. 94.

## Chapter Six

1. Holbrook Jackson, *The Eighteen Nineties*, p. 229.
2. "False theory and the Theatre," *Fancies versus Fads*, p. 130.
3. "Boredom of the Butterflies," *ibid.*, p. 121.
4. "A Defence of Penny Dreadfuls," *The Defendant* (London, 1901), p. 20.
5. The story is related in Ward, *Gilbert Keith Chesterton*, p. 252.
6. See "The Secret of Father Brown" in the collection of that name, for a contrast of the two detectives.
7. "The Duel of Dr. Hirsch," *The Wisdom of Father Brown*, p. 272.
8. "The Hammer of God," *The Innocence of Father Brown*, pp. 174–75.
9. "The Oracle of the Dog," *The Incredulity of Father Brown*, pp. 498–99.
10. "The Dagger with Wings," *The Incredulity of Father Brown*, pp. 580–81.
11. *The Innocence of Father Brown*, pp. 18–22.
12. "The Man with Two Beards," *The Secret of Father Brown*, p. 682.
13. *The Coloured Lands* (New York, 1938), p. 107.
14. R. A. Knox, "Chesterton in his Early Romances," *Dublin Review* (October, 1936), p. 354.
15. William R. Titterton, *G. K. Chesterton: a Portrait*, p. 45.
16. *The Napoleon of Notting Hill* (London, 1961), p. 99.
17. *The Club of Queer Trades* (London, 1960), p. 32.
18. "The Man Who Was Thursday," *G.K.C. as M.C.*, p. 205.
19. Dedicatory poem, "To Edmund Clerihew Bentley," *The Man Who Was Thursday* (New York, 1960), n.p.
20. "The Man Who Was Thursday," *G.K.C. as M.C.*, p. 205. Ronald Knox characterizes all of the early novels as dreams ending in nightmares. See "Chesterton in his Early Romances," pp. 351–65.
21. "Ego et Shavius Meus," *The Uses of Diversity*, p. 160.
22. "The Man Who Was Thursday," *G.K.C. as M.C.*, pp. 205–6.
23. *The Return of Don Quixote* (New York, 1927), p. 286.
24. For the "literature of invasion," see Samuel Hynes, *The Edwardian Turn of Mind*, p. 34 ff.

25. Chesterton said: "I could not be a novelist; because I really like to see ideas or notions wrestling naked, as it were, and not dressed up in a masquerade as men and women." *Autobiography,* p. 298.

## Chapter Seven

1. *Selected Essays* (New York, 1950), p. 248.
2. Compare Chesterton's dictum that the artist "does not express his personality." "The Mirror," *Lunacy and Letters,* pp. 90–93.
3. Ward, *Gilbert Keith Chesterton,* p. 371.
4. *The Wild Knight of Battersea,* p. 40. Lea credits Chesterton with being one of the first to attempt the rehabilitation of Pope in this century (p. 52).

## Chapter Eight

1. Margaret Clarke, "Chesterton the Classicist," *Dublin Review,* CCXXIV (First quarter, 1955), pp. 51–67.
2. On occasion he termed himself a "romantic person," but he was using the word in the sense of "light-hearted, impractical, or nonsensical." "On Phases of Eccentricity," *All I Survey,* p. 68.
3. He confesses he is one of the many poets of antiquity who failed to see the beauties of Nature. "The Poetry of Cities," *Lunacy and Letters* (New York, 1958), p. 21. Like Dr. Johnson he hears the Lord in the "still small voice of Fleet Street." "The Surrender of a Cockney," *Avowals and Denials,* p. 16.
4. Northrop Frye, *A Study of English Romanticism* (New York, 1968), pp. 4–15.
5. For the "transcendent belief" in morality during the Victorian age, see Gertrude Himmelfarb, *Victorian Minds* (New York, 1968), p. 302 ff.
6. *Heretics,* p. 7.
7. Ward, *Gilbert Keith Chesterton,* p. 209.
8. Bernard Bergonzi, "Chesterton and/or Belloc," *The Critical Quarterly,* I (Spring, 1959), p. 67.
9. Hugh Kelly, S. J., "G. K. Chesterton: His Philosophy of Life," *Studies* (March, 1942), p. 86.
10. *Paradox in Chesterton,* pp. 2–4.
11. "Preface" to Walter S. Masterman, *The Wrong Letter* (London, 1926), p. v.
12. "The Appetite of Earth," *Avowals and Denials,* p. 59.
13. *On the Place of Gilbert Chesterton in English Letters,* p. 41.
14. "On Jonathan Swift," *All I Survey,* pp. 83–84.

15. "A Defence of Dramatic Unities," *Fancies versus Fads,* p. 114.

16. "A Glimpse of My Country," *Tremendous Trifles,* p. 285.

17. "The Architect of Spears," *A Miscellany of Men,* p. 250.

18. "Science and Religion," *All Things Considered,* p. 140.

19. Michael Mason, *The Centre of Hilarity* (London, 1959), pp. 12–13 and 176–83.

# Selected Bibliography

No uniform or definitive edition of Chesterton's work exists, and the closest approximation is the nine-volume Minerva Edition of The Library Press (1926). Dufour Editions of Philadelphia has initiated a Chesterton Reprint Series that has reached seven volumes at this writing.

The bibliographical problem facing any writer on Chesterton is enormously simplified by John Sullivan's *G. K. Chesterton: a Bibliography* (University of London Press, 1958); words are inadequate to explain the usefulness of this fine research tool.

The items in this bibliography are the editions used in preparing this book; the date in parentheses is that of the first edition where it differs from that of the edition used.

PRIMARY SOURCES

1. Major works: Fictions, Collections of Essays, Studies, Plays, Poetry (arranged in alphabetical order)

*Alarms and Discursions.* New York: Dodd, Mead and Co., 1911. (1910)
*'All I Survey.'* London: Methuen and Co., 1933.
*All is Grist.* New York: Dodd, Mead and Co., 1932. (1931)
*All Things Considered.* New York: Sheed and Ward, 1956. (1908)
*The Appetite of Tyranny. Including Letters to an Old Garibaldian.* New York: Dodd, Mead and Co., 1915 (Includes *The Barbarism of Berlin*)
*Appreciations and Criticisms of the Works of Charles Dickens.* London: J. M. Dent and Sons, and New York: E. P. Dutton and Co., 1911.
*As I Was Saying.* New York: Dodd, Mead and Co., 1936.
*Autobiography.* New York: Sheed and Ward, 1936.
*Avowals and Denials.* London: Methuen and Co., 1938. (1934)
*The Ball and the Cross.* New York: John Lane Co., 1909.
*The Ballad of St. Barbara.* London: Cecil Palmer, 1922.
*The Ballad of the White Horse.* London: Methuen and Co., 1911.
*The Barbarism of Berlin.* London: Cassell and Co., 1914.
*The Catholic Church and Conversion.* New York: The Macmillan Co., 1961. (1927)

*Charles Dickens.* New York: Schocken Books, 1965. (1906)

*Chaucer.* London: Faber and Faber, 1958. (1932)

*Christendom in Dublin.* London and New York: Sheed and Ward, 1933. (1932)

*The Club of Queer Trades.* London: Darwen Finlayson, 1960. (1905)

*The Collected Poems.* London: Cecil Palmer, 1927 (reprinted, New York: Dodd, Mead and Co., 1966).

*The Coloured Lands.* New York: Sheed and Ward, 1938.

*Come to Think of It.* New York: Dodd, Mead and Co., 1931. (1930)

*The Common Man.* London: Sheed and Ward, 1950.

*The Crimes of England.* London: Cecil Palmer and Hayward, 1915.

*Culture and the Coming Peril.* London: University of London Press, 1927.

*The Defendant.* London: R. Brimley Johnson, 1901.

*Divorce versus Democracy.* London: The Society of Saints Peter and Paul, 1916.

*The End of the Armistice.* New York: Sheed and Ward, 1940.

*The End of the Roman Road.* London: The Classic Press, 1924.

*Eugenics and Other Evils.* London: Cassell and Co., 1922.

*The Everlasting Man.* New York: Doubleday and Co., 1955. (1925)

*Fancies versus Fads.* New York: Dodd, Mead and Co., 1923.

*The Father Brown Omnibus.* New York: Dodd, Mead and Co., 1933.

*Five Types.* London: Arthur L. Humphreys, 1912.

*The Flying Inn.* New York: Sheed and Ward, 1956. (1914)

*Four Faultless Felons.* London: Cassell and Co., 1930.

*G. F. Watts.* London: Duckworth and Co.; New York: E. P. Dutton and Co., 1904.

*G.K.C. as M.C.* London: Methuen and Co., 1929.

*Generally Speaking.* London: Methuen and Co., 1928.

*George Bernard Shaw.* New York: Hill and Wang, 1956. (1909)

*The Glass Walking-Stick.* London: Methuen and Co., 1955.

*Greybeards at Play: Literature and Art for Old Gentlemen.* London: Sheed and Ward, 1930. (1900)

*A Handful of Authors.* London: Sheed and Ward, 1953.

*Heretics.* London: The Bodley Head, 1960. (1905)

*The Incredulity of Father Brown.* London: Cassell and Co., 1926.

*The Innocence of Father Brown.* London: Cassell and Co., 1911.

*Irish Impressions.* New York: John Lane Co., 1920. (1919)

*The Judgement of Dr. Johnson.* London: Sheed and Ward, 1930. (1927)

*Lunacy and Letters.* Ed. Dorothy Collins. New York: Sheed and Ward, 1958.

*Magic: A Fantastic Comedy*. New York: G. P. Putnam's Sons, 1914.
(1913)

*The Man Who Knew Too Much*. Philadelphia: Dufour Editions, 1963.
(1922)

*The Man Who Was Thursday: A Nightmare*. New York: G. P.
Putnam's Sons, 1960. (1908)

*Manalive*. London: Thomas Nelson and Sons, 1912.

*A Miscellany of Men*. London: Methuen and Co., 1926. (1912)

*The Napoleon of Notting Hill*. London: The Bodley Head, 1961.
(1904)

*The New Jerusalem*. New York: George H. Doran Co., 1921. (1920)

*Orthodoxy*. London: The Bodley Head, 1957. (1908)

*The Outline of Sanity*. London: Methuen and Co., 1926.

*The Paradoxes of Mr. Pond*. London: Cassell and Co., 1937.

*Poems*. London: Burns and Oates, 1915.

*The Poet and the Lunatics*. New York: Dodd, Mead and Co., 1929.

*The Queen of Seven Swords*. London: Sheed and Ward, 1933. (1926)

*The Resurrection of Rome*. London: Hodder and Stoughton, 1930.

*The Return of Don Quixote*. New York: Dodd, Mead and Co., 1927.

*Robert Browning*. London: Macmillan Co., 1964. (1903)

*Robert Louis Stevenson*. New York: Dodd, Mead and Co., 1928.
(1927)

*St. Francis of Assisi*. New York: Doubleday and Co., 1957. (1923)

*St. Thomas Aquinas*. New York: Doubleday and Co., 1956. (1933)

*The Scandal of Father Brown*. New York: Dodd, Mead and Co., 1935.

*The Secret of Father Brown*. New York: Dodd, Mead and Co., 1927.

*A Short History of England*. New York: John Lane Co., 1917.

*Sidelights on New London and Newer York*. London: Sheed and
Ward, 1932.

*The Spice of Life*. Ed. Dorothy Collins. Philadelphia: Dufour Editions, 1966.

*The Superstition of Divorce*. London: Chatto and Windus, 1920.

*The Superstitions of the Sceptic*. Cambridge, England: W. Heffer
and Sons; St. Louis: B. Herder Co., 1925.

*The Surprise*. London: Sheed and Ward, 1952.

*Tales of the Long Bow*. New York: Dodd, Mead and Co., 1925.

*The Thing*. London: Sheed and Ward, 1929.

*Tremendous Trifles*. New York: Dodd, Mead and Co., 1915. (1909)

*Twelve Types*. London: Arthur L. Humphreys, 1910. (1902)

*The Uses of Diversity*. London: Methuen and Co., 1920.

*Utopia of Usurers*. New York: Boni and Liveright, 1917.

*Varied Types*. New York: Dodd, Mead and Co., 1909. (1908)

*The Victorian Age in Literature.* London: Oxford University Press, 1966. (1913)

*The Well and the Shallows.* New York: Sheed and Ward, 1935.

*What I Saw In America.* New York: Dodd, Mead and Co., 1922.

*What's Wrong With the World.* London: Cassell and Co., 1912. (1910)

*The Wild Knight.* London: Grant Richards, 1900.

*William Blake.* New York: E. P. Dutton and Co., 1910.

*William Cobbett.* New York: Dodd, Mead and Co., 1926. (1925)

*The Wisdom of Father Brown.* London: Cassell and Co., 1914.


2.   Selected minor works: contributions, introductions, etc.

*The Characteristics of Robert Louis Stevenson.* With W. Robertson Nicoll. New York: James Pott & Co., 1906.

*Charles Dickens.* With F. G. Kitton. New York: James Pott & Co. [n.d.].

*Charles Dickens Fifty Years After.* Privately printed by Clement Shorter. London, 1920.

*A Chesterton Calendar.* London: Kegan Paul, Trench, Trubner and Co., 1911.

"Dickens and Thackeray," *The Outline of Literature.* Ed. John Drinkwater. Vol. III. New York: G. P. Putnam's Sons, 1924.

"Do We Agree?" A Debate between G. K. Chesterton and Bernard Shaw with Hilaire Belloc in the Chair. Hartford, Connecticut: Edwin Valentine Mitchell, 1928.

"Gilbert and Sullivan," *The Eighteen-Eighties. Essays by the Fellows of the Royal Society of Literature.* Ed. Walter de la Mare. Cambridge: the University Press, 1930.

"How to Help Annexation." London: Hayman, Christy, and Lilly Co., 1918.

"I Say a Democracy Means . . ." New York: privately printed, 1941.

"Introduction," *G.K.'s: A Miscellany of the First 500 issues of G. K.'s Weekly.* New York: Coward McCann, 1935.

"Introduction." William Cobbett. *Cottage Economy.* London: Peter Davies Ltd., 1926.

"Letters to an Old Garibaldian." London: Methuen and Co., 1915.

*Leo Tolstoy.* With G. H. Perris and Edward Garnett. London: Hodder and Stoughton, 1904.

"Lucifer, or the Root of Evil," *If I Could Preach Just Once.* New York: Harper and Bros., 1929.

*Lord Kitchener.* London: Horace Cox Ltd., 1917.

"Mary Queen of Scots," *Revaluations: Studies in Biography.* London: Oxford University Press, 1931.

*Tennyson.* With Richard Garnett. London: Hodder and Stoughton, 1903.

*Thomas Carlyle.* With John E. Hodder Williams. London: Hodder and Stoughton, 1903.

"William Cobbett." *Essays by Divers Hands.* Being the Transactions of the Royal Society of Literature of the United Kingdom. Ed. Frederick S. Boas. London: Humphrey Milford, 1923.

"Why I am a Catholic," *Twelve Modern Apostles.* New York: Duffield and Co., 1926.

SECONDARY SOURCES

1. Biographical and Historical

BELLOC, HILAIRE. *The Servile State.* New York: Henry Holt and Co., 1946. Analysis of the modern secular state; throws light on Chesterton's social criticism.

BENTLEY, EDMUND CLERIHEW. *Those Days.* London: Constable and Co., Ltd., 1940. Informal memoirs by one of Chesterton's best friends at St. Paul's.

BIRKENHEAD, FREDERICK EDWIN SMITH, 1ST EARL OF. *Famous Trials of History.* Garden City, N. Y.: Garden City Publ. Co., 1926. Legal view of the Marconi trial, as told by "Chuck It" Smith.

BRAYBROOKE, PATRICK. *I Remember G. K. Chesterton.* Epsom: Dorling and Co., Ltd., 1938. Detailed memoirs of the author's dealings with Chesterton. Unreliable.

CHESTERTON, ADA E. *The Chestertons.* London: Chapman and Hall, 1941. Cecil's wife tells the story of two brothers and their marriages; intemperate in her dislike of Frances.

CLEMENS, CYRIL. *Chesterton as Seen by his Contemporaries.* Webster Groves, Mo.: International Mark Twain Society, 1939. The testimony of a number of literati and friends of Chesterton; very useful accounts of his visits to the United States, and his lectures and debates here.

DANGERFIELD, GEORGE. *The Strange Death of Liberal England, 1910–1914.* New York: Capricorn Books, 1961. Informal account of the period; emphasizes the Parliamentary maneuvering and the feminist movement.

GRAVES, ROBERT and ALAN HODGE. *The Long Weekend: A Social History of Great Britain, 1918–1939.* Brisk, amusing narrative of the fads, manias, and traumas of Great Britain between the wars.

HALÉVY, ELIE. *History of the English People in the Nineteenth*

*Century*. Volumes V and VI. New York: Barnes and Noble, Inc., 1961. Standard history of the period.

HYNES, SAMUEL. *The Edwardian Turn of Mind*. Princeton: Princeton University Press, 1968. Useful, if somewhat disconnected, group of essays on some aspects of the period.

JACKSON, HOLBROOK. *The Eighteen Nineties: A Review of Art and Ideas at the Close of the Nineteenth Century*. London: Grant Richards Ltd., 1922. Still the best study of the personalities and squabbles of the *fin de siécle*.

*Mark Twain Quarterly, The* (Special G.K.C. issue), Vol. I, No. 3 (Spring, 1937). A number of personal appreciations.

O'CONNOR, JOHN. *Father Brown on Chesterton*. London: Burns Oates and Washbourne, Ltd., 1938. Important memoirs by "Father Brown" on their meeting, their friendship, and Chesterton's conversion.

RECKITT, MAURICE B. *As It Happened*. London: J. M. Dent and Sons, 1941. Includes the story of Reckitt's work with Chesterton in the Distributist Cause and with *G. K.'s Weekly*.

TITTERTON, WILLIAM R. *G. K. Chesterton: a Portrait*. London: Alexander Ouseley Ltd., 1936. Important memoirs discuss the work of the Distributist League and the formation of *G. K.'s Weekly*.

TUCHMAN, BARBARA. *The Proud Tower: A Portrait of the World before the War, 1890–1914*. New York: Bantam Books, 1967. Colorful history of the pre-war period; especially useful for the French intellectual background.

WARD, MAISIE. *Gilbert Keith Chesterton*. New York: Sheed and Ward, 1943. The indispensable biography which makes full use of notebooks, letters, and personal memoirs of friends.

—————. *Return to Chesterton*. London: Sheed and Ward, 1952. Supplements the large biography with additional memoirs, letters, documents; particularly helpful on working habits and friendships with children.

2.  Critical

AGAR, HERBERT. "A Great Democrat," *The Southern Review*, III (Summer, 1937), 95–105. Underscores GKC's feelings that man-made instruments and organizations must be maintained at a human scale.

BELLOC, HILAIRE. "Gilbert Chesterton." *One Thing and Another*. London: Hollis and Carter, 1955. A brief essay (developed fully in the next item) on his friend's logic and constant appeal to reason.

—————. *On the Place of Gilbert Chesterton in English Letters*.

London: Sheed and Ward, 1940. Important interpretation by a lifelong companion; emphasizes the precision of thought and lucidity of Chesterton; votes for *The Thing* as the best piece of work.

BERGONZI, BERNARD. "Before 1914: Writers and the Threat of War," *The Critical Quarterly*, VI (Summer, 1964), 126–34. Chesterton was one of many who foresaw the coming of the second World War.

––––––. "Chesterton and/or Belloc," *The Critical Quarterly*, I (Spring, 1959), 64–71. An interesting attempt to judge the stature of the two contemporaries; finds Chesterton more genial, but remote today because of a "too rationalistic" imagination.

BISHOP, JOHN. "G. K. Chesterton: Man of Letters and Defender of the Faith," *London Quarterly Review*, CLXXIII (April, 1948), 149–55. Chesterton seen less as a thinker than as a dealer in tastes and intuitions.

BOGAERTS, ANTHONY M. A. *Chesterton and the Victorian Age.* Hilversum: Rosenbeek En Venemans Uitgeversbedr. N.V., 1940. A doctoral dissertation on an important subject; unfortunately prosaic and often misleading.

BRADBROOK, B. R. "The Literary Relationship between G. K. Chesterton and Karel Capek," *Slavonic and East European Review*, XXXIX (June, 1961), 327–38. Capek influenced by Chesterton's paradoxes and materials in the Father Brown stories.

BRAYBROOKE, PATRICK. *Gilbert Keith Chesterton*. Philadelphia: J. B. Lippincott Co., 1922. Series of essays, often appreciative and argumentative; to be used with care.

––––––. *The Wisdom of G. K. Chesterton.* London: Cecil Palmer, 1929. Another series of essays giving us more of Braybrooke than of Chesterton; very selective and superficial.

BROWN, IVOR. "A Multiple Man," *The Observer*, April 16, 1944. Sees Chesterton's political essays of permanent value; annoyed by the "glorious haze of ignorance" present elsewhere.

BULLETT, GERALD. *The Innocence of G. K. Chesterton.* London: Cecil Palmer, 1923. Very unsympathetic; finds him naïve in religion; incapable of creating fiction of permanent value.

CAMMAERTS, EMILE. *The Laughing Prophet: The Seven Virtues and G. K. Chesterton.* London: Methuen and Co., 1937. Sympathetic tracing of the major Christian virtues in personality and writings.

CARTER, HUNTLY. "Chesterton on the Moscow Stage," *The Outlook*, March 8, 1924. Interesting description of a Moscow stage production of *The Man Who Was Thursday* which claimed to discover a strong strain of collectivism in Chesterton's thinking.

(CHESTERTON, CECIL). *Gilbert K. Chesterton: A Criticism.* New York: John Lane Co., 1909. Important early discussion of the central ideas of London's literary lion; surprisingly disapproving.

CLARKE, MARGARET. "Chesterton the Classicist," *Dublin Review,* (1st Q, 1955), 51–67. Explains briefly the Christian form of humanism adopted by the mature writer.

DE BLACAM, AODH. "Defender of the Faith: Chesterton's First Conversion," *The Irish Monthly,* LXXIII (January, 1945), 47–55. First of his spiritual crises was the discovery of a sort of "mystical materialism."

EAKER, J. GORDON. "G. K. Chesterton among the Moderns," *The Georgia Review,* XIII (Spring, 1959), 152–60. Once Chesterton accepted the "Thomistic theory of Being" everything he said was predictable.

EDWARDS, DOROTHY. "G. K. Chesterton," *Scrutinies: Critical Essays by Various Writers.* Ed. Edgell Rickword. London: Wishart and Co., 1928. Very unsympathetic; seen as "cocksure" about his ideas, and so seems "far worse than a liar."

ERVINE, ST. JOHN G. "G. K. Chesterton," *Some Impressions of My Elders.* New York: The Macmillan Co., 1922. Stresses focus on "the common man" that helps one retain his balance.

EVANS, MAURICE. *G. K. Chesterton.* Cambridge: The University Press, 1939. Brief, excellent summary of main philosophical position (particularly his struggle against pessimism); glances at the artistry of his novels, essays, and poems.

FLANAGAN, THOMAS. "Amid the Wild Lights and Shadows," *Columbia University Forum,* I (Winter, 1957), 7–10. Praises Chesterton's use of the detective story as a "kind of poem."

FREEMAN, JOHN. "G. K. Chesterton: A Canterbury Pilgrim," *London Mercury,* IV (August, 1921), 392–403. Angry about Chesterton's "obstinately static mind" and flippant style.

GASSMAN, JANET. "A Second Look at G. K. Chesterton," *Religion in Life,* XXVIII (Summer, 1959), 443–54. Concerns fight against the mechanized, depersonalized life of modern man.

GILKES, A. N. "G. B. S., G. K. C. and Paradox," *Fortnightly Review,* CLXXIV (October, 1950), 266–70. Finds Chesterton's use of "paradox contradictory" superior to the type used by Shaw.

GREEN, V. H. H. "Gilbert Keith Chesterton. I. The Challenge of the Age," *Theology,* XLIII (August, 1941), 93–101. Rebellion is of primary importance in understanding him.

————. "II. The Response of G.K.C.," *Theology,* XLIII (September, 1941), 150–55. Christian humanism was an effective substitute for the godless materialism around him.

HANDSACRE, ALAN (pseud. for Albert C. White). *Authordoxy: Being a Discursive Examination of Mr. G. K. Chesterton's "Orthodoxy."* London: John Lane, the Bodley Head, 1921. Fair, if unsympathetic, examination of the weak points in Chesterton's logic; thoroughly committed to science and rationalism as against religion.

HARDIE, W. F. R. "The Philosophy of G. K. Chesterton," *Hibbert Journal,* XXIX (April, 1931), 449–64. Stresses the strong moral impetus in his works; wisely points out that much of his philosophy is not specifically Catholic but humanist. Excellent analysis.

HART, JEFFREY. "In Praise of Chesterton," *Yale Review,* LIII (May, 1964), 49–60. Argues that his thought is essentially political, and that the prose style is surprisingly concentrated.

HOLLIS, CHRISTOPHER. *Gilbert Keith Chesterton.* London: Longmans Green and Co., 1954. Excellent brief introduction to the man and his works.

————. *The Mind of Chesterton.* Coral Gables, Fla.: University of Miami Press, 1970. An important Catholic interpretation which is marred, however, by an excess of apologetics, the chronological organization, and curious proportions.

————. "Prophet of the Counter-Attack," *The Listener,* November 25, 1948. Appreciative essay; stresses the connection between "The Ballad of the White Horse" and Belloc's *The Servile State.*

JONES, W. S. HANDLEY. "G. K. Chesterton and the Discovery of Christianity," *London Quarterly Review,* CLXXIII (October, 1948), 324–32. Emphasizes the strong sense of normality; also his belief that all of man's systems should be made for man.

KELLY, HUGH. "G. K. Chesterton: His Philosophy of Life," *Studies* (March, 1942), 83–97. Chesterton's exuberance was always restrained within conservative limits; a sharp contrast exists between his style and his substance.

KENNER, HUGH. *Paradox in Chesterton.* New York: Sheed and Ward, 1947. Most detailed study of Chesterton's style, his analogical perception, and the theological foundation for paradox. Very important.

KNOX, RONALD A. "Chesterton in his Early Romances," *Dublin Review,* XCIX (October, 1936), 351–65. Largely on the romances and their ideological burden. (Reprinted in *Captive Flames: A Collection of Panegyrics.* London: Burns Oates, 1941.)

————. "Father Brown," *Literary Distractions.* New York: Sheed and

Ward, 1958. Admires the mood, atmosphere, and settings in the detective stories.

KUNKEL, FRANCIS L. "The Priest as Scapegoat in the Modern Catholic Novel," *Ramparts*, I (January, 1963), 72–78. Father Brown's "exterior struggles" are less profound than the tormented lives of the fictional priests of Georges Bernanos and Graham Greene.

LAS VERGNAS, RAYMOND. *Chesterton, Belloc, Baring*. Trans. C. C. Martindale. New York: Sheed and Ward, 1938. Finding reason insufficient, Chesterton moved to faith in a "hilarious God," and a religion of "good news."

LEA, F. A. *The Wild Knight of Battersea*. London: James Clarke and Co., 1945. Perhaps the wisest brief treatment of Chesterton available; concludes that his "vision is imaginative, his expression of it intellectual."

LEVIN, BERNARD. "Pantomime Horse," *The Spectator*, December 5, 1958, pp. 833–34. Finds Belloc superior to Chesterton, but both inaccessible because "they were romantics, and we are not."

LEWIS, C. S. "Notes on the Way," *Time and Tide*, November 9, 1946, pp. 1070–71. Defends Chesterton against James Stephens's charge that he is seriously dated.

LOWTHER, F. H. "G. K. Chesterton: The Man and his Work," *London Quarterly Review*, CLXVIII (October, 1943), 335–41. His works were incurably autobiographical; religious emotion was the impetus for all he wrote.

LUNN, ARNOLD. "G. K. Chesterton," *Roman Converts*. London: Chapman and Hall, 1925. Basically unsympathetic; concludes Chesterton prevented him from discovering a truly plausible case for Catholic doctrine.

LYND, ROBERT. "Mr. G. K. Chesterton and Mr. Hilaire Belloc," *Old and New Masters*. London: 1919. Finds both writers mainly inspired by the "medievalist spirit."

SISTER MARIE VIRGINIA, S.N.D. *G. K. Chesterton's Evangel*. New York: Benziger Brothers, 1937. Long appreciation of the religious inspiration behind Chesterton's works.

MASON, MICHAEL. *The Centre of Hilarity*. London: Sheed and Ward, 1959. Indispensable, provocative defense of Chesterton as a synthesis of the "common and clerkly" strains of modern literature (best represented by D. H. Lawrence and T. S. Eliot); his love of existence interpreted as the heritage for all future writers.

MUGGERIDGE, MALCOLM. "GKC," *New Statesman*, August 23, 1963, p. 226. Sees him as a frustrated, anguished spirit beneath the boisterous cheerfulness.

NOYES, ALFRED. "The Centrality of Chesterton," *Quarterly Review*

(January, 1953), pp. 43–50. A romantic compared to Dr. Johnson; fundamentally a poet.

PALMER, HERBERT E. "G. K. Chesterton and his School," *Post-Victorian Poetry*. London: J. M. Dent and Sons, 1938. Finds a surprising amount of good poetry in all that he wrote, and places him at the head of a "school."

PFLEGER, KARL. "Chesterton, the Adventurer of Orthodoxy," *Wrestlers with Christ*. Trans. E. I. Watkin. London: Sheed and Ward, 1936. Presents the highly personal form of orthodoxy Chesterton discovered for himself: "His everlasting theme is man."

RAYMOND, JOHN. "Jeekaycee," *The New Statesman*, LIII (March 23, 1957), 384–85. Finds Chesterton a "distressingly homogeneous" writer—not a great social prophet.

RECKITT, MAURICE B. "G. K. Chesterton: A Christian Prophet for England Today," *The World and the Faith: Essays of a Christian Sociologist*. London: The Faith Press, 1954. Sensitive description of the malaise afflicting modern man and Chesterton's solutions. Very good.

————. "Belloc and Chesterton: Study of an Impact," *The World and the Faith*. (See entry above.) Comparison of two personalities and their mutual influence.

SCOTT, WILLIAM T. *Chesterton and Other Essays*. New York: Eaton and Mains, 1912. Two essays stress his pugnacity and his ability to "scent out" the main idea of a work.

SHAW, GEORGE BERNARD. *Pen Portraits and Reviews*. London: Constable and Co., 1932. Four reprinted pieces comment with wit on Chesterton's obviously unShavian ideas; the first, "The Chesterbelloc: a Lampoon" (Reprinted from *The New Age*, February 15, 1908) describes that "formidable animal" presently rampaging in merry England. Recommended.

SLOSSON, EDWIN. "G. K. Chesterton," *Six Major Prophets*. Boston: Little, Brown, and Co., 1917. Flippant, unsympathetic impressions of philosophy and novels.

STEPHENS, JAMES. "The 'Period Talent' of G. K. Chesterton," *The Listener*, XVIII (October 17, 1946), 513–14. Unsympathetic; particularly about "Lepanto."

VERSFELD, M. "Chesterton and St. Thomas," *English Studies in Africa*, IV (March, 1961), 128–46. Rather thin treatment of an important subject; makes clear how the "image" became the foundation of any philosophy in both men.

WARD, WILFRED. "Mr. Chesterton among the Prophets," *Men and Matters*. London: Longmans, Green and Co., 1914. Defends Chesterton against the charge of lack of seriousness.

WARING, HUBERT. "G.K.C.: Prince of Essayists," *Fortnightly Review*, 148 (ns. 142), (November, 1937), 588–95. Sees him at his best in the essay and poem; is too thoroughly a propagandist to write a good story.

WELLS, H(ERBERT) G(EORGE). "About Chesterton and Belloc," *An Englishman Looks at the World*. London: Cassell and Co., 1914 (Reprinted from *The New Age*, January 11, 1908.). Arguments against the Distributism—and anti-Socialism—of his two opponents.

WEST, JULIUS, G. K. *Chesterton*. New York: Dodd, Mead and Co., 1916. Praises the prose style and comic poems; unsympathetic toward the religious and political views. To be used with caution.

WILLIAMS, CHARLES. "G. K. Chesterton," *Poetry at Present*. Oxford: Clarendon Press, 1930. Poetry is full of "the voice of battle" because, like Milton, he sees man as a fighting animal.

WILLS, GARRY. *Chesterton, Man and Mask*. New York: Sheed and Ward, 1961. Stresses the psychological conflict of "realism" and solipsism; often opaque and misleading. To be used with caution.

WILSON, EDMUND. "Meetings with Max Beerbohm," *Encounter*, XXI (December, 1963), 16–22. More on Max; finds Chesterton unreadable today because of his "mechanical and monotonous" style.

# Index

187